102 & 104 Leibniz

112 quote from Berkeley

173 Kant

THE HISTORY OF THE CONCEPT
OF ASSOCIATION OF IDEAS

The History
of the Concept of
Association of Ideas

DAVID RAPAPORT

INTERNATIONAL UNIVERSITIES PRESS, INC.

NEW YORK

Manufactured in the United States of America

Contents

Preface—Solomon E. Asch   vii

The History of the Concept of Association
  of Ideas   1

Bacon: The Psychological Foundations
  of Induction   7

Descartes: The Beginnings of Skepticism   21

Hobbes: The Origins of Mechanistic Psychology   35

Spinoza: Toward a Psychological Analysis
  of Mysticism   48

Locke: The Borderland of Sensualism and
  Empiricism   66

Leibniz: The Metaphysical Phylogenesis of
  Being and the Unconscious   86

Berkeley: Solipsistic Idealism Without
  Abstract Ideas   107

Hume: The Birth of Skepticism and Positivism   122

Kant: The Transcendental Deduction
  of Categories   160

Summary   180

Reference Notes   186

Preface

THE PROBLEM of associations is inextricably linked with the history of psychological thought. It was under this rubric that thinkers first identified phenomena and issues that continue to be alive today. After emerging in ancient Greece, the notion of association reappeared in the modern period, at first almost casually; but gradually it gathered force, became a powerful current, and at times the key principle of psychological systems. Despite many vicissitudes this development has continued down to the present; indeed, much that has happened in psychology during this century either carries forward or is a reaction against doctrines of association. No serious inquiry into the human mind can ignore this concept.

The growth of the idea of association makes an absorbing and instructive story. A construction of outstanding minds who undertook to chart the ways of human thinking, it brings before us one of the first attempts at a coherent psychological theory. At certain periods associationism was not only the major, but the sole theory of order in the mental domain. It is revealing to follow the formulation of problems in their nascent form, before more specialized concerns and accumulations of detail have begun to obscure a larger view. Aside from its intrinsic interest, the historical record places current concerns in a fresh, often illuminating perspective. That much of the early history of this movement is today not well understood only enhances the value of the present study.

This, the first substantial work of David Rapaport but the latest of his writings to be published, was a doctoral dissertation he submitted in 1938 to the faculty of the University of Budapest. Except for those who knew the author personally, its existence was unknown to the psychological community. Studies of this genre are usually slated for oblivion; what saves the present work from this fate is the psychological talent and the personal flair that the author brought to his task. His inquiry foreshadowed a concern that marked Dr. Rapaport's subsequent contributions: to explore the continuities in psychological thinking that might help overcome its fragmentation. To his aid came a sympathetic imagination that enabled him to steep himself in the vision and insights of each thinker. The reader will find in this monograph more than a recital of past views. Contributing to its vitality was a determination to uncover latent themes that might furnish guides for the future.

The present monograph spans the seventeenth and eighteenth centuries, a period of less than two hundred years that from the vantage point of the present belongs to the "prehistory" of psychology. During this period the first tentative steps were taken toward a psychology of association. Those who are not inclined to dismiss past ideas as outmoded will make a number of unexpected discoveries. Most notably they will find that the contemporaries and immediate successors of Descartes, Spinoza, and Locke considered association within a frame of reference strikingly different from that of later psychology.

Their paramount concern was epistemological: they attempted to clarify the sources and possibilities of valid knowledge. It was this concern that prompted them to raise questions about human thought, and it was in this setting that they turned to the problems of association. Association itself was incidental to their inquiries, not the central issue it was to become later. This intellectual horizon had altered drastically when psychology began to emerge as a separate discipline about one hundred years ago. As a consequence of new currents—among them the doctrine of evolution and the rise of an experimental tradition—the earlier epistemological interests shifted notably; indeed the very notions of knowledge and truth underwent a profound change in psychology.

Given their starting point, the earlier thinkers focused on the relation of association to understanding. Dr. Rapaport's account makes clear that they encountered a serious problem at this point: associations, they found, do not provide the insight and evidence they assumed to be necessary to understanding. Moreover, associations are often a source of error that disturbs correct thinking. Although sequences of associations correspond to the order of events in the world (including that of inner experiences), these reflect merely factual regularities. Further, since these correspondences are often based upon contingent conjunctions of events, they can become the foundation of false beliefs. Thus there arise disparities between the necessities of reasoning and the accidents of personal experience that determine the course of associations.

These limitations probably discouraged a more detailed exploration of associative operations. They clashed with Descartes' search for clear and distinct ideas as the necessary foundation of knowledge. Thus Descartes, having sketched a physiological account of associations, relegated them to bodily functioning; they played little part in his treatment of thinking. Spinoza's monism produced a more moderate conclusion; he regarded associations as incomplete thoughts, but he distinguished sharply between them and adequate understanding. And John Locke, strangely considered by some a founder of the doctrine of associations, singled them out as the main source of human unreasonableness, a sort of madness of normal persons. Locke chose what we nowadays call emotional conditioning as the prototype of association. Not only were such "false connexions" often irrational, but they could not be cured by reasoning. The labyrinth of associations, so often productive of confusion and chaos, hardly seemed a promising point of departure when the primary concern was with the difference between true and false. Clearly these philosophers did not underestimate association as an obstacle to true knowledge; reasoning was for them a function not reducible to association.

In contrast to this rationalistic theme, British empirical philosophy introduced a radically different perspective on knowledge. David Hume, the commanding figure and culmination of this movement, proposed a startling account of the limitations of human understanding; to support it he relied on a psychological analysis of associative operations. Hume maintained that relations of cause and effect were not accessible to understanding; judgments concerning relations between facts were consequences solely of association by contiguity and similarity. Such associations generated causal expectancies and beliefs under the pressure of instinctive tendencies that could not be justified on logical grounds. Although Hume only reasserted the shortcomings of association earlier thinkers had discerned, he also claimed to have shown that appeals to understanding were futile. With this step he decisively augmented the import of associative activities; the fortunes of association rose as those of reason fell. Hume altered the climate of thinking for subsequent psychology and envisioned conceptions that were to become significant much later. In him one finds the germs of the view that associations are the basis of the universal laws of thinking, that the same principles account for correct and incorrect thinking, and an emphasis on the continuities of mental functioning in animals and men. Although Hume strictly excluded logical and mathematical judgments from his critical analysis, he prepared the way for the lifting of this barrier in later ages.

Despite the importance of their ideas, it is helpful to realize that what the thinkers under discussion had to say about association was cursory rather than exhaustive. They did not specify what they meant by association beyond referring to a few everyday examples. However, the context of their writings makes it clear that they were working with an inclusive rather than a narrow notion of association, one that embraced all mental transitions "from this to that." When they first considered the phenomena of association they were seeking a key to the organization of the mind, to its most deeply hidden ways. Here is doubtless the reason for the spell the idea of association exerted through the centuries: it referred to the entire restless flow of mental life the study of which promised to disclose its innermost secrets. Dr. Rapaport fully realized this concern in the thinkers he studied. He was near enough to them in spirit to share the conviction that knowledge was a supreme good and to wonder how it could be freed of error. This quest fascinated him, imbuing his inquiry with a sense of excitement and challenge.

Dr. Rapaport's study stops well before the elaboration of systematic theories of association, and before the formation of associationistic schools of psychology. Consequently, many themes that were to become prominent in the future do not form part of his account. The nineteenth and twentieth centuries took the study of association in new directions revealing strong links with the past but also major departures. British empirical philosophy continued to provide the intellectual foundations. Atomism and the premise that knowledge derives solely from experience became central to the introspective and behavioristic movements. Association acquired an unprecedented importance under these auspices; thus the investigation of learning became virtually coextensive with the topic of association. On the other hand, concern with cognitive processes suffered erosion; the view that thinking is to be traced to primitive and confused origins acquired an almost unchallenged obviousness. Yet this century also saw the most determined questioning of the tenets of associationism. Gestalt psychology provided a fundamental critique and an alternative interpretation of associations, as did the more recent developments in linguistic theory. In a very real sense, psychology stands nearer today to its seventeenth-century predecessors than it has during the last two hundred years.

Dr. Rapaport has brought vividly before us a formative period in the history of psychology the study of which can only deepen understanding of its present problems.

The task he faced was not easy, given its scope and the lack of substantial historical scholarship in psychology. Much remains to be done in exploring the long and complex story. What he did also belongs, of course, to its time and place. This is the work of a young man filled with enthusiasm, with an unquestioned sense of the importance of the past for the present. He provides a link with ideas that had largely disappeared from the psychological horizon. What he had to say preceded his direct contact with American psychology; thus he himself stood at a crossroads in his development. The work abounds in penetrating insights. One cannot fail to see that his inquiry was oriented to the future and was very much part of a personal quest. This book is a beginning, but what David Rapaport left undone others will be in a better position to continue given the example of his utter respect for the labors of the past.

Had David Rapaport lived, he might have revised this work, but it seemed appropriate not to tamper with what he left. The reader owes a debt to Mrs. Elvira Strasser Rapaport who discovered a draft of the English-language translation (by L. Juhasz) and edited it, and who checked all quotations and references.

SOLOMON E. ASCH
University of Pennsylvania
January 1974

The History of the Concept of Association of Ideas

THE HISTORY of the concept of association, like any other history of concepts, may be divided into two stages. During the first stage, the facts forming the subject of the future concept are not yet consciously recognized. In the second stage, the interplay of these facts becomes clearer and their conscious use gradually emerges, thus allowing the development of precise terminology.

The history of a certain concept is difficult to trace after these stages have been completed. The need to review the history of the concept is usually first felt when, in the course of its historical career, it has become part of public usage, thus endangering its scientific adequacy in that definition is replaced by public consciousness and a variety of concepts are reduced to one common denominator. A review also may be in order when new investigations extend the apparently well-established scope of the concept in order to give it a certain flexibility or a new scope and definition or to substitute for it another concept and definition better suited to interpreting the available data.

Today we have reached a stage in the history of the

concept of association where such a review appears imperative. The concept of association has become vulgarized and, as a commonly used notion, rendered devoid of meaning. New researches have assailed its legitimacy. New facts have come to light that cannot be explained by the classic concept of association.

This point of departure for the present study is offered by a historical situation. The guiding principle of our thesis is to outline the conceptual history of association in such a way as to let the historical continuity emerge and to let the unity of philosophy, epistemology, and psychology be seen to be pointing the way for the new psychology, thus ending the present chaos clouding the problem of association.

The chapter in the history of association concepts comprised in the present work encompasses modern philosophy from Bacon to Kant. In their time, associations as phenomena became gradually known and were crystallized as a definite concept (Locke), and the concept reached the climax of its ramifications and variability (Hume). Thus this period occupies a place of perhaps crucial importance in the history of the concept of association.

After this period, the problem of associations passes from the domain of philosophy to become a subject matter of psychology. The legacy of English association psychology was in turn inherited by physiological psychology (Wundt, Ziehen). The reaction sets in with experiential psychology (*Erlebnis-Psychologie*)—the first protest against the general significance of associations. At the same time, Ebbinghaus and G. E. Müller subjected associations, learning, and will to close examination. Their findings began a chain of researches that culminated in the experimental methods of Lindworsky, Selz, Ach, and Lewin. These researches thoroughly refuted the classic theory of associations. They were later completed by the successive examination of those special psychic functions it had been customary to subsume under the explanatory classification of associations. Thus, Köhler and his students subjected the problems of "successive comparisons" and the "blurring of impressions with time" to experimental analysis. These researches also ran counter to the theory of associations.

Simultaneously with the development of modern psychology there arose specialized branches that approached the subject of associations from many sides. It was started by ethnopsychology, which first identified associations with the prelogical patterns of thinking found among primitive people (Lévy-Brühl). But later, the magical and animistic patterns of thinking having been discovered, this science was confronted with problems that could not satisfactorily be solved by the aid of the then-prevailing concept of association. In child psychology, pathopsychology, animal psychology, etc.—in short, in the whole of comparative psychology—a similar situation arose.

Psychoanalysis made associations the focus of its method. Freud, in his *Interpretation of Dreams* (27), described in detail the nature of associations he discovered, and Jung devoted a series of investigations to the problem.

In Pavlov's reflexology and in the empirical viewpoint of behaviorism—the trial-and-error formula (Thorndike, Tolman)—associations were given a decisive role. On the other hand, Buytendijk's, Üxküll's, and Lorenz's animal psychology propounded an opposing theory: adjustment of the animal to its environment is based on its instinc-

· 3

tive a priori attitudes and, besides learning, on its spontaneous perception of the "signal" qualities of the environment. This theory did not accept learning by associations in the form just mentioned.

Gestalt psychology regards associations as nonessential external forms behind which stand the gestalten (Köhler, Wertheimer, Koffka).

One could list here a number of other approaches and numerous systems of modern philosophy taking a positive or negative view of the subject. Associations indeed represent a real problem in our day.

The struggle among these opposing directions in psychology centers on the relationship of man and animal to their respective environments. According to Pavlov, man's manifestations of life are conditioned reflexes brought about by associations. The behaviorists assert that living beings purposively adjust to their environment through trial and error. According to the Gestalt theory man and animal possess the necessary discernment to grasp the gestalt having relevancy to their environment. In Freudian doctrine man is driven by instinctive urges, which shape the external world for his consciousness, while the resistant part of the external world, which frustrates instinctual wishes, forms the ego and its sense of reality. According to the animal psychologists, there is an initial relationship between the animal and its environment, which, in Üxküll's words, is as strong as the bond between the animal and its body parts.

Thus, in the problem of the relationship between a living being and its environment we recognize the problem of existence and consciousness. The solution of the problem of association is linked to the solution of this problem.

Contemporary psychology faces the task of reconciling these conflicting experimental data and theories. The present study is intended as a contribution to the formation of a concept of association unifying the varied results of speculation and experiment.

Our task is to show what problems have been linked with the concept of association in the history of philosophy and to retrace the course they have taken therein. This includes the issue of how and to what extent the results arrived at or suggested by psychology are components or trends in the history of philosophy.

This scope of our investigation posed new demands as far as methodology is concerned. We had to construct a history of one—psychological—component of philosophical systems, namely, the concept of association. Accordingly, we had to look at and reconstruct not the logical but the psychologic-genetic developments in these systems of philosophy. This resulted in a seeming neglect of the speculative-metaphysical aspects of the systems under scrutiny and a focus on the genetic-psychologic elements. But nothing was farther from my purpose than such a value judgement. The psychological component was brought to the fore because our research intended to shed light on just this problem.

The employment of the psychological method, by dint of its unusual nature, made it necessary to support every step in our study by quotations from the respective authors or from their most authoritative interpreters. This was required in order to validate my method. I refrained from this only in the first part of the chapter on Kant, since the problems under scrutiny there are the subject of secular dispute. The pages, paragraphs, and chapters quoted refer to the editions listed in the bibliography.

The conceptual history of associations preceding the periods under study may be outlined as follows:

1. The trains of thought of cosmogonies and mythologies suggested the existence of associations.

2. Vestiges of mnemotechnical devices used by the peoples of antiquity show that they were aware of the role of associations.

3. Greek, Indian, and Chinese philosophies attained—more or less explicitly—the theoretical level whence Bacon and Descartes take their departure. Scholasticism added a few ideas to the Greek heritage but without progress in the conceptual-historical line. Bacon and Descartes pick up the thread almost precisely where Greek and Hellenistic philosophies dropped it.

With Descartes and Bacon the conceptual history of associations is started on the road leading up to the present. From here on we will follow it in detail.

Bacon: The Psychological Foundations of Induction

I

IN MODERN PHILOSOPHY associations are first encountered in Bacon's "idols." Bacon thought that the human mind is hindered in the recognition of the true laws of human nature by four idols, which he described as follows:

> The idols of the den are those of each individual; for everybody (in addition to the errors common to the race of man) has his own individual den or cavern, which intercepts and corrupts the light of nature, either from his peculiar and singular disposition, or from his education and intercourse with others, or from his reading, and the authority acquired by those whom he reverences and admires, or from the different impressions produced on the mind, as it happens to be preoccupied and predisposed, or equable and tranquil, and the like; so that the spirit of man (according to its several dispositions) is variable, confused, and, as it were, actuated by chance; and Heraclitus said well that men search for knowledge in lesser worlds, and not in the greater or common world [(6) I, 42].

The *idols of the den* arise from the peculiar mental or somatic constitution of each individual and also from education, habit, and accident ([6] I, 53).

Lastly, there are idols which have crept into men's minds from the various dogmas of peculiar systems of philosophy, and also from the perverted rules of demonstration, and these we denominate idols of the theatre: for we regard all the systems of philosophy hitherto received or imagined, as so many plays brought out and performed, creating fictitious and theatrical worlds. Nor do we speak only of the present systems, or of the philosophy and sects of the ancients, since numerous other plays of a similar nature can be still composed and made to agree with each other, the causes of the most opposite errors being generally the same. Nor, again, do we allude merely to general systems, but also to many elements and axioms of sciences which have become inveterate by tradition, implicit credence, and neglect. We must, however, discuss each species of idols more fully and distinctly in order to guard the human understanding against them [(6) I, 44].

The *idols of the theatre* are not innate, nor do they steal into the understanding secretly; they are plainly impressed on and received into the mind from the play-books of philosophical systems and the perverted rules of demonstration ([6] I, 61). Idols of the theatre, or of systems, are many, and there can be and perhaps will be many more ([6] I, 62). These are the results of man's reverence of authority and his belief in "theatrical stories."

There are also idols formed by the reciprocal intercourse and society of man with man, which we call
idols of the market, from the commerce and association of men with each other; for men converse by
means of language, but words are formed at the will
of the generality, and there arises from the bad and
unapt formation of words a wonderful obstruction to
the mind. Nor can the definitions and explanations
with which learned men are wont to guard and protect
themselves in some instances afford a complete remedy; words still manifestly force the understanding,
throw everything into confusion, and lead mankind
into vain and innumerable controversies and fallacies
[(6) I, 43].

But the *idols of the market* are the most troublesome
of all—idols that have crept into the understanding
through the alliances of words and names. For men
believe that their reason governs words: but it is also
true that words influence understanding ([6] I, 59).

The idols of the tribe are inherent in human nature
and the very tribe or race of man; for man's sense is
falsely asserted to be the standard of things; on the
contrary, all the perceptions both of the senses and the
mind bear reference to man and not to the universe,
and the human mind resembles those uneven mirrors
which impart their own properties to different objects,
from which rays are emitted and distort and disfigure
them [(6) I, 41].

The *idols of the tribe* have their foundation in human
nature itself and in the tribe or race of men. For it is a

false assertion that the sense of man is the measure of things. On the contrary, all perceptions, of the senses as well as of the mind, are according to the measure of the individual and not according to the measure of the universe ([6] I, 13).

According to Bacon, man injects these idols into every real relationship. He supplants the real relationships by those determined by the idols. He connects the facts and objects of the external world, that is, associates with them. Training, custom, and chance cause these concepts to be grouped in men's minds, and they retain their respective positions in later life. Facts are arranged in a certain sequence and connected in some pattern by acknowledged authority, and the connections and relationships posited by them affect men with the force of compulsion when, in scientific researches, they try to arrange all results in accordance with them instead of seeking to obtain and make use of facts as they are. And often words are connected with things according to the judgement of the market-place of the masses ([6] I, 59). Thus, as a result of incorrect use of words, radically different things are lumped together.

So we can see that, in substance, idols are associations brought about under influences, brought about by different causes. This is clearly shown already in the first three idols. The fourth one merits particular attention. It is in fact both a prerequisite and summation of all the others: it is inherent in human nature to suppose that man is the measure of things. In this the very essence of idols is expressed: that when man believes the permanent connections (associations) created in his own subjective imagination to be real connections in the external world

—that is, when he believes himself to be the measure of things—he is worshipping an idol!

Bacon presented the formation of associative connections as a general attribute of human nature. So far only their negative effects and significance have been stressed. Perhaps it is not too soon to assert that, though the positive aspects of associations contributed significantly to the development of Bacon's philosophy, the next chapter in the conceptual history of associations was influenced primarily by the negative aspects. The historical role of the Baconian method of induction will bear out this statement. The fact is that associations were introduced into modern philosophy through Bacon's negative interpretation of their role. Descartes resumes these researches; and through him they are inherited by Locke, who—while examining these "destructive" associations—formulates the concept of *assotiatio idearum* (the connection of ideas).

II

Bacon stands on the dividing line between scholasticism and modern philosophy. In his entire system one can observe the dualism of the weighty heritage of the past and of the germinating seeds of the future. This dualism is reflected in the idols, too. Bacon's entire ideology turns against scholasticism and above all against Aristotelianism; this is an important facet in his ideology. One recognizes this in the idol of the theater—that is, of the respect for authority. However, the anti-Aristotelian trend plays only a negative part, and Bacon's system makes use of it only dialectically. The positive, the experiential, component is represented by the other idols. The opportunity and internal necessity for his opposition to scholasticism and Aristotelianism could have been occasioned by positive and experience-inspired events. The futility of scholastic disputes suggested to him the idols of the human mind. The blind respect for authority is just one among these. The system of idols is the experience-inspired basis which supplies him with a feeling of inner security in opposing scholasticism. This is the epistemological significance of the idols in Bacon's system and of the Baconian association theory for us. Equipped with these ideas he turns against teleology:

> There are and can exist but two ways of investigating and discovering truth. The one hurries on rapidly from the senses and particulars to the most general axioms, and from them, as principles and their supposed indisputable truth, derives and discovers the intermediate axioms. This is the way now in use. The other constructs its axioms from the senses and particulars, by ascending continually and gradually, till it finally arrives at the most general axioms, which is the true but unattempted way [(6) I, 19].

Then he resumes the discussion of his views on teleology and he leaves no doubt that he sees their origin in psychic factors. "The mind strives after that which is most general, in order to rest there: for it soon gets tired of experience." Even in our day thinkers are tempted to assume this attitude. Bacon formulated the opinion elsewhere with greater emphasis: "The ancient authors, from particular instances and by the aid of a few well known ideas and the most pleasing tenets, rose to the most general conclusions of science" ([6] I, 14).

If we compare these views with the doctrine of the idols, we easily comprehend the origins of the teleological bent of the human mind. For, ere any one fact appears, we already have our ready-made idols, to be joined (associated) to those facts by force of custom, authority, training, and terminology. Thus, idols supply the motive force of teleology.

But Bacon discredited these attributes of the human mind. "It is rightly laid down that true knowledge is that which is deduced from causes" ([6] II, 2). However, the final cause even corrupts the sciences, except in the intercourse of man with man (*ibid.*). Man indeed measures the facts he encounters by his life goals—Bacon the statesman knew this from personal experience. But for science, which does not orient itself to life goals, this is harmful, since "man is not the measure of things." And Bacon virtually summarizes the experience-inspired nature of idols and their effects on science:

The human understanding is most excited by that which strikes and enters the mind at once and suddenly, and by which the imagination is immediately filled and inflated. It then begins almost imperceptibly to conceive and suppose that everything is similar to the few objects which have taken possession of the mind, whilst it is very slow and unfit for the transition to the remote and heterogeneous instances by which axioms are tried as by fire, unless the office be imposed upon it by severe regulations and a powerful authority [(6) I, 47].

In what epoch of the history of science have there not been known such procedures? What thinking man has not had difficulty realizing that the inner dynamism of his thinking activity, his wish-guided ideas and associations, distort reality? Bacon was fully aware of this psychological fact and even pointed out the associative dynamism of its formation. Our last quotation bears witness to the fact that he even had some knowledge of how desires and the imagination influence our thoughts and theories. This idea is present in germinal form throughout the conceptual history of association. Expounding it would be synonymous with supposing that associations are guided by appetitive factors. This notion did arise in the course of history, but it attained clear formulation only after Kant.

Thus we have gained the following description of the psychogenesis of teleology: It is an inherent property of the human mind to try to find referents *for each experience* in inherited and acquired notions and connections. This jump means that man supposes all phenomena to be arranged in accordance with a priori given—because inherited and acquired—final causes. The instruments of the arrangement are the idols (associations). And the meaning of the idols and their criticism serve the epistemological aims of the criticism of teleology. As a conclusion to his exposition, Bacon finally stated:

> . . . he who contemplates nature should suspect whatever particularly takes and fixes his understanding, and should use so much the more caution to preserve it equable and unprejudiced [(6) I, 58].

Nor can we suffer the understanding to jump and fly from particulars to remote and most general axioms. . .We must not. . . add wings, but rather ballast to the understanding, to prevent its jumping or flying, which has not yet been done. . . [(6) I, 104].

III

Associations gained positive significance in the foundation of the inductive method. By his method of perfecting induction gradually, Bacon himself forged the "ballast" that was to hinder the human mind from "jumping and flying." The underlying principle of the method is characterized by him in the following passage:

. . . man's present industry has hitherto been active and curious in noting the variety of things, and explaining the accurate differences of animals, vegetables, and minerals, most of which are the mere sport of nature, rather than of any real utility as concerns the sciences. Pursuits of this nature are certainly agreeable, and sometimes of practical advantage, but contribute little or nothing to the thorough investigation of nature. Our labor must therefore be directed towards inquiring into and observing resemblances and analogies, both in the whole and in parts, for they unite nature, and lay the foundations of the sciences [(6) II, 27].

This notion recurs in Spencer's doctrine. The search for similarities and identities still left open the road to nomology and associative links between concepts. But Bacon's point of departure, the quest after the "form" and the *tabulae*, which were chosen as the method, link up this first scientific theory of induction with associations. Windelband ([5] I, p. 145) remarked that it is "this inference by analogy"—that is, the associative method—"by which his genius, with the aid of a lucky insight, broke the limits of his method, to seek its way toward a universal view." The basis of the *tabulae*, which constitute the method of Baconian induction, is indeed this analogical method—the seeking of similarities.

Bacon wished to collect in the *tabula praesentiae* all the phenomena in which the property under examination or one similar to it is manifested. (In the *Novum Organum* he chooses heat as an example.) In the *tabula absentiae* he describes all those phenomena in which that property is missing or in which its very opposite is present. But compiling lists of similarities and identities is an effort of subjective validity only. No guarantee of correctness in terms of natural law can be attached to this method. We should not be surprised then if many things that have nothing to do with heat manage to get into these tabulae. The *tabula absentiae* brings even more extravagant results: here purely associative connections interfere strongly with the conclusions. Such are the focalization of the heat of opaque warm bodies or the cold light of the moon and of the stars.

So far Bacon's system leads to the very results it ascribes to scholasticism, although more methodically. However, this is only seemingly so. Bacon employs the associative method merely for collecting data. The facts gathered are examined further in a *tabula gradui*. This investigation shows that *absentia* and *praesentia* are relative insofar as they have degrees, gradations. By successive exclusion, he eliminates the irreconcilable data and interpretations. Thus, he looks for agreement in the associatively obtained material on a higher level. He tests the results so gained against "prerogative instances" to see whether they can be used successfully to interpret those examples. But these prerogative instances are again merely associatively obtained "similar" cases. Hence the experience provided by them cannot in any way decide the validity of the results of induction. Bacon again faces the problem of similarities of form, after having tried —during the lengthy process of induction—to eliminate teleology and the false appearances created by the associatively produced *tabulae*. This clearly shows that the elimination of associations will remain a vain hope as long as we do not know their real nature. Bacon only recognized their idol-like effect. His achievement constituted a starting point in English psychologism in that it opposed these idols and the teleology that is their natural accompaniment, while laying the foundations of induction, the origin of positivism. Psychic activity and the role of associations in it were not clarified in Bacon's work. Even in creating the four types of idol in human nature, he stayed within the limits of the scholastic theory of forms. He did not even succeed in formulating a theory of mechanism based on his discoveries about human nature. This was accomplished by his disciple Hobbes. Yet, there is evidence that Bacon was aware of the importance of associations not only as obstacles to true knowledge but as a fundamental function of the mind. This is apparent from Book II, Chapter 26 of *Novum Organum*, which deserves our attention also because it gives repeated expression to the fundamental notion of induction. The fifth eminent example is being discussed:

In the fifth rank of prerogative instances, we will class constitutive instances, which we are wont also to call collective instances. They constitute a species of lesser form, as it were, of the required nature. For since the real forms (which are always convertible with the given nature) lie at some depth, and are not easily discovered, the necessity of the case and the infirmity of the human understanding require that the particular forms, which collect certain groups of instances (but by no means all) into some common notion, should not be neglected, but most diligently observed. For whatever unites nature, even imperfectly, opens the way to the discovery of the form. The instances, therefore, which are serviceable in this respect, are of no mean power, but endowed with some degree of prerogative.

Here, nevertheless, great care must be taken that, after the discovery of several of these particular forms, and the establishing of certain partitions and divisions of the required nature derived from them, the human understanding do not at once rest satisfied, without preparing for the investigation of the great or leading form. . . [(6) II, 26].

The first results are the clusters under consideration that have been connected by nature, even though imperfectly. As an example, Bacon cites the functioning of the faculty of remembering.

He describes how the memory classifies and arranges its own material. The instruments of this ordering are the natural locations in which we see objects and which facilitate their recall. We can easily remember things when they are associated with well-known personalities or symbols. Orderly arrangement aids the memory; we use this method with animals and plants. Initial letters and words aid memorizing. Great personalities, contemporary or historical, also serve as useful points of reference. In general, every grouping into clusters helps the work of memory; it is in fact a function of the memory, by which we connect a less memorable incident to a more convenient and notable one. Thus, we learn poetry easier than prose. If we connect the abstract with the concrete, the former tends to be remembered with greater facility. Events related to strong emotions (shame, fright, amazement, etc.) will be the better retained. Texts arranged in sections or read aloud can be retained with greater ease. Things awaited with expectation are retained longer than those we just register. Generally, each grouping separates the object to be retained from the infinite; this decidedly aids memory and increases its natural power.

There is no need to demonstrate that these instruments of the memory are all associative bonds. What is surprising is only that, for Bacon, they remain "instruments" as far as both knowing and the memory are concerned. The budding induction of natural science was not ready to apply its methodology and its conviction in the existence of universal regularity to the psyche. But the theory of induction, although it chose a teleological path, bestowed on us a doctrine of permanent value. The essence of it, which to this day constitutes a treasure of natural science, may be summed up as follows.

We collect phenomena of similar type—that is, those associatively connected (cf. [6] I, 45, 46, 47). On the basis of their similarity, ubiquity, or frequency, we set up generalizations (induction), which we contrast with one another in "crucial experiments" ([6] II, 36) and thus gradually crystallize into theory, which is the highest level of generalization.

In conclusion, it should also be pointed out that Bacon, who thought that the intrinsic bias of the human mind ascribes too much similarity and uniformity to nature, necessarily closely approximated a skeptic position when he designated the search for similarities and associative links as the first stage of induction. For here he was not far from assuming that science in its entirety is but the offspring of man's natural tendency to seek out conformities and identities. He was rescued from such a conclusion by a tradition of empiricism inherited from Vives, Ramus, Valla, and L. Pico. But his own experiences led him to the same assumption. He clearly stated that the goal of science was to render humanity wealthier and happier (cf. [1] p. 120). We will have occasion to observe that philosophers, influenced by their perception of associations, often are tempted to paddle them into the epistemological backwaters of skepticism. With Bacon it was the favorable current of empiricism that helped him stay out of those backwaters; with Spinoza, it was mystical intuition; with Descartes, pure rationalism. These facts allow us to cast a penetrating glance into the inner dynamism and semantic relativity of philosophical concepts.

Bacon, then, fought against the influence of associations but did not reject them; instead he made them the instruments of his own inquiry. He substituted the inductive method, which gradually filtered out the unreal contents of associations to replace a teleology founded on the influence of idols and associations.

Descartes: The Beginnings
of Skepticism

———————

I

THE SIGNIFICANCE of associations in psychic life
according to Descartes can be outlined in a few sen-
tences:

> Thus, when the soul desires to recollect something,
> this desire causes the gland, by inclining successively
> to different sides, to thrust the spirits toward different
> parts of the brain until they come across that part
> where the traces left there by the object which we wish
> to recollect are found; for these traces are none other
> than the fact that the pores of the brain, by which the
> spirits have formerly followed their course because of
> the presence of that object, have by that means ac-
> quired a greater facility than the others in being once
> more opened by the animal spirits which come towards
> them in the same way [(2) 13].

In this Descartes relied entirely on Plato's memory
engram theory.

And besides that, if this figure is very strange and frightful, that is, if it has a close relationship with the things which have been formerly hurtful to the body, that excites the passion of apprehension in the soul and then that of courage, or else that of fear and consternation according to particular temperament of the body or the strength of the soul [(2) 36].

This proposition contains two known associative connections. First, that two similar experiences may substitute for each other and may bring about each other's effect. Second, that experiences and affects may be associated; that is, the occurrence of one experience may bring with it another which had previously elicited a given effect.

Thus when we see the light of a flame or hear the sound of a bell, the sound and the light are two different actions that, solely by giving rise to two different motions in some of our nerves, and by their motions in the brain, give two different sensations to the mind which we transpose to the object which is supposed to be the cause of them that we think we see the flame itself and hear the bell, and not to feel only motions that come from them [(2) 23].

Here Descartes recognized the associations of the whole and its parts. This is all Descartes could tell us about the classic concept of association. He viewed associations as products of the physiological functions of the human body. Psychic phenomena, the passions, memory, etc.— with the exception of the highest faculties of judgement— result from this physiological process; associations become the basis of the physiological foundations of psychology. If we did not wish to learn more about Descartes, our researches, ignoring a few obscure and equivocal details, could terminate here. We could still maintain that Descartes was aware of the phenomenon of associations. He thought that there was a *mechanical* connection between the psychic past and psychic present. The chain leading from Plato and Aristotle through the principal advocates of scholasticism and which reappeared with Bacon was not severed with Descartes. On the contrary, in his philosophy associations regained the importance Aristotle had secured for them. While associations resulted only in epistemological consequences in the Baconian doctrine, Descartes founded his whole psychology on them. But this is only a "somatic" psychology, for Descartes ascribed these laws to the "*substantia extensa.*" Thus the unity of psychic life cannot be achieved by the Cartesian method. Psychology is stuck at the *res extensa.* The laws of the *res cogitans*—or reason—are unrelated to them. Acquainted with his studies, we can say, although we have only initial proof, that Descartes probably took the essentials of his theory of associations from scholasticism. He gave a consistent mechanistic interpretation to the earlier merely analogical and presumptive imprint-of-the-memory (engram) theory. He laid down its physiological foundations and created a suitable hypothesis which, with the aid of the same laws, could be empirically verified and developed. In the second place, realizing the connection between experiences and passions, this rationalistic philosopher anticipated the perspectives that became fundamental later in Schopenhauer, then in positivistic philosophy, and finally in Freudian psychology. This realization is not fortuitous in

Descartes' system; on the contrary, it is its necessary complement. In Section 51 of *Passions of the Soul* he said the motions of vital forces are the cause of the passions. By specifying these motions, he built a theory of the whole of affective psychic life. That is, Cartesius, whose aim was to deliver the psychic from material or quantitative qualities, became the virtual founder of a psychic energetics. This energetics is a forerunner of the Freudian libido doctrine. This is what we learn directly from Descartes about the associations.

II

I would like to try to go beyond Descartes' conceptually formulated opinion to learn more about it, and, from the place of this opinion in his entire system of philosophy, to see what he knew and thought about associations. Let us consider again the third quotation: the pealing of the bell conjures up the bell for us, the light of the flame reminds us of the flame itself—this is association. The bell and its sound, the flame and its light usually present themselves to us simultaneously. Sound and light recall bell and candle. But here we must pause! Because it is just here that Descartes' philosophy of doubting sensory experience—*"de omnibus dubitandum"*—originated: "I observed that these [the senses] sometimes misled us; and it is the part of prudence not to place absolute confidence in that which we have even once been deceived by" ([4] p. 220). What could this disenchantment refer to when Descartes' definition of sensory experience is what has just been quoted? I think it legitimate to suppose that the phrase "the senses . . . misled us" refers to the deceptive nature of associations. To support this pro-

position I quote some hitherto rather obscure passages of
Passions of the Soul:

> Of the perceptions caused by the body, most depend
> on the nerves; but there are some among them that do
> not depend on these, called images, as well as those of
> which I have just spoken, from which they neverthe-
> less differ, in that our will does not contribute to their
> formation, and consequently they cannot be listed
> among the activities of the mind. They are created
> when the vital forces, moving in different ways in the
> brain, hit on the traces of former impressions and thus
> they are directed rather toward these than other pores
> of the brain [(4) 21].

> It remains to be remarked that everything the mind
> perceives by the mediation of the nerves may be pre-
> sented to it by a fortuitous movement of the vital forces.
> Such disappointments do not present themselves in
> the case of the passions, for these are so close to our
> soul and they are so intimate that it can feel them
> only as in reality [(4) 26].

> [The passions] may also be called perceptions when
> we use this word in a general sense to mean all the
> thoughts that do not belong to the activity of the soul
> or of the will; but nevertheless not in cases when it is
> used to mean evident knowledge . . . One can also call
> them sensations, by the fact that they are received in
> the mind in the same way as the objects of external
> sensations [(4) 28].

After the supposition given above, these quotations
assume a new meaning. Apparently, we cannot trust such

sensations as are capable of being produced by the stichic movements of vital forces. (For Descartes these are the ill-defined or undefined cases, in which the other side of the mechanistic theories comes to the fore.) And if conceptions of a somatic origin and among them the passions—the only connecting link between the body and the mind in the Cartesian system—also intervene, then merely obscure and chaotic images can ensue. Thus all somatically based experiences are at the mercy of the blind play of associations, and Descartes had every reason to pronounce his caveat: *de omnibus dubitandum.*

Before discussing the epistemological conclusions Descartes arrived at from the abovementioned premises, I will have to consider one more facet of the problem which points the way toward the future. The obscurity of concepts having a somatic basis implicitly contains the problem of the unconscious. Ever since Leibniz, this question has been often raised; in the nineteenth century it was a universal concomitant of psychological and associative investigation. Psychophysics can avoid this pitfall only by equating the psychic and the conscious in order to give associations the central mechanistic significance they have in that system and to eliminate the concept of the unconscious from psychology. In this matter, Descartes virtually forestalls those modern doctrines in which the unconscious plays a role analogous to the vegetative nervous system and is so to speak the "voice of the organism" (W. R. Hess, Pötzl).

III

What, then, remained for Descartes that was true and not deceptive? In other words, what were the epistemological consequences of these influences of associations?

We find the answer in Sections 43, 44, and 45 of the *Principles of Philosophy:* "*But it is certain we will never admit falsity for turth, so long as we judge only of that which we clearly and distinctly perceive.*" And he calls clear that which is "*present and manifest to the mind giving attention to it*" and distinct that "*which is so precise and different from all other objects as to comprehend in itself only what is clear*" ([4] pp. 331–332).

These assertions themselves, but above all the definition of the concept of *distinctness*, point to the fact that by them he wishes to extricate that which he regards as true from the complex of disturbing associations which do not distinguish between the thing or concept under consideration and other things or concepts but, on the contrary, connect them with all other things and concepts. The "present manifest" is clarified if, in accordance with our supposition, we complete it as *present to the mind and not substituted by another concept.* Thus the associations have deceived us—they mixed perceptions with other perceptions and resulted in misconceptions. Consequently, Descartes recognized concepts as true only if they are sharply separated from others and are present to the mind.

In the *Principles of Philosophy* he lists some frequently encountered types of such associative connections. These are noteworthy precisely because he takes them from Bacon; and Locke, in his turn, incorporates them in his *Essays.* When creating the concept of "*associatio idearum,*" Locke had these examples in mind. Thus, in Book I, Section 71, he lists as one of the main sources of error the wrong associations originating from childhood. These, he says, stay with us "in our mature years, when the mind [is] no longer wholly subject to the body" ([4] p. 329); for even if we know that they are mistaken, it is very difficult to eradicate them. Descartes calls these connections prejudices. Then he points out that when we concentrate our attention on objects not present to us, our mind becomes weary and consequently we judge according to prejudice and not the present impression. Finally, the incorrect linking of concepts and words also results in error, for we commit concepts to memory as connected with words; namely, when we "attach our thoughts to words which do not express them with accuracy" ([4] p. 332).

IV

What is the source of clear and distinct ideas, of true judgements? Meditation 11 of *Meditations on the First Philosophy* contains those tenets that have been made immortal in the proud formula *cogito ergo sum.* Their essence is that even if everything deceives me and everything is a mistake, the existence of the self still remains a fixed point. This is indubitable; for even if an enemy of unlimited power deceived me on this, he says with sophisticated sagacity, "I exist, since I am deceived; and let him deceive me as he may, he can never bring it about that I am nothing . . ." ([4] p. 220).

Translated into the terms of our hypothesis, this maxim reads: Our concepts of objects are deceiving because the intervention of associations confuses them with earlier concepts which had been made an integral part of the organism and had left their mark on the brain; even though the self is confused by such notions, at least they are its own. Thus this process becomes an introspective activity of the self. (This sounds like a precursor of Fichte's and Schelling's thought.)

Windelband had pointed out earlier:

Peculiarly enough, this great spirit never revealed the depth of those disappointments that are inherent in the concepts we form about ourselves. On the contrary, he started out from the supposition that there is nothing simpler and more lucid than this most complicated and compressed of our concepts; and he wanted to shed light on our knowledge from the dark background of our mental life [(5) p. 182].

Thus it becomes understandable that Descartes does not stop at this point. In the second part of *Meditations* and, as Cassirer (1) shows, in several of his letters and in *Notae in programme quoddam*, Descartes designates the *ideae innatae* as a source of such clear and distinct ideas. This is consistent with the foregoing. If the self is to comprehend itself, it must at the very least possess an inherent order that is independent of chance connections.

Descartes formulates his view at the end of the second part of *Meditations*: "It is now manifest to me that bodies themselves are not properly perceived by the senses, nor by the faculty of imagination, but the intellect alone." In May 1643 he addresses Princess Elisabeth thus:

We all carry in us the pure basic concepts which are to be held original and by which we form all later experience. . . . Among them there are those that are of general validity for the various classes and problems, for example existence, number, duration; others pertain to bodies only, such as space, form, movement; and thinking has validity only for the soul [translated from the text].

Commenting on this passage, Cassirer (1) remarks that these doctrines were developed from Cusanus' theory of assimilation.

Descartes described the *ideae innatae*, the concepts expressing absoluteness and relativity, in *Regulae VI*. Here we get a more complete picture than the one referred to above. Absolute ideas are those of cause, simplicity, universality, unity, equality, similarity, and rectilinearity. Relative ones are effect, composition, partiality, multiplicity, inequality, dissimilarity, and obliqueness. Later these emerge in the psychologies of association as the creating fields of associations and in Kantian philosophy as certain elements of categories.

The problem of the *ideae innatae* is rooted in Plato's theory of anamnesis, the relationship of which to knowledge is analogous in the Platonic dialectics to the problem of association. This problem also lays the foundations for a priori categories of knowing and the category of pure reason.

I should like to point out here that Descartes, while settling the problem of knowledge in this manner also raises, and in his way settles, the question of the constancy of objects and of concept formation. It is important to note that in the later philosophies, but especially in modern psychology, the same questions appear in exactly the same frame of reference as with Descartes.

V

In the fourth part of *Meditations* Descartes again undertakes the interpretation of errors. Since we are trying to form a judgement on the theory of associations in Descartes' philosophy by considering his philosophical starting point, we have to compare our conclusions with his own to see whether they fit the same pattern. If they do not, our attempt will have been unsuccessful. Descartes says:

> I observe that these (my errors) depend on the occurrence of the causes, viz. the faculty of cognition which I possess and that of election, or the power of free choice—in other words, the understanding and the will. For by the understanding alone, I neither affirm nor deny anything, but merely apprehend (*percipio*) the ideas regarding which I may form a judgement; nor is any error properly so called, found in it thus accurately taken [(4) p. 252].

> Whence, then, spring my errors? They arise from this cause alone, that I do not restrain the will, which is of much wider range than the understanding, within the same limits, but extend it even to things I do not understand, and as the will is of itself indifferent to such, it readily falls into error and sin by choosing the false in place of the true, and evil instead of good [(4) p. 254].

> As often as I restrain my will within the limits of my knowledge, that it form no judgement except regarding objects which are clearly and distinctly represented to it by the understanding, I can never be deceived [(4) p. 257].

Descartes defined the will and reason in Section 17 of *Passions of the Soul* as follows: "Will is the active, reason the passive state of the soul." If we remark about Descartes' idea of reason, with Cassirer, that "it is no more influenced by objects than are the rays of the sun hurt by objects they light upon," it becomes clear that reason is self-immanent and is but an unchanging and unchangeable frame of innate ideas, being thus necessarily without error on the basis of what has already been asserted. In contrast, the will is the principle of activity, and as such it always comes into contact with the body— and through it, with the external world. But it does not choose from among clear mental propositions, for such are not to be found there. It gets entangled in the quagmire of associations. There was but one thing Descartes could recommend as salutary for the activity of the mind he himself created: to return to its brother, pure reason; for an army of errors await it on the outside. The returning will is then made to oppose the external world—and doubts. Thus it appears that our hypothesis follows Descartes' system closely wherever they come into contact.

VI

In conclusion I have to point out that the majority of the new schools of psychology, physiology, and biology see the archenemy in the Cartesian system. All their efforts are directed at liberating psychology from what they consider the spell under which it has languished for centuries (Buitendyk, E. Straus, Weizsäcker, Bühler, Hull). What are these efforts trying to combat?

The recognition of the mind-body dichotomy has a long history. Yet philosophy had to take great pains to crystallize this dichotomy, because to men of former ages it was no clearer than the other qualities of the undifferentiated individuality. This dichotomy was not crystallized even during the long process of individuation; and in part it is still obscure. Our researches concerning the reciprocal effects and coexistence of mind and body have progressed tremendously, but their solution is still unfathomably remote. It is only natural that this aim, not attainable for generations to come, should have occasioned serious tensions and that, at crucial periods of science, the tension became almost intolerable. Descartes' historical position coincides with one of these turning points. The tension was unbearable. The particularized sciences, advancing at a snail's pace, which were to bring some attenuation, could not satisfy Descartes' eagerness to obtain a unified perspective and stand up to the magnitude of the challenge indicated by the tension. For Descartes, the originators of the tension were the age of skepticism in which he lived and the age of scholasticism from whose culture his mind had sprung. Thus, this universal spirit had to be his own measure. He severed the tie between the two poles, separating body and mind to relax the tension.

Physiological psychology, created by Descartes, centered on the concept of the motion of vital forces and of the associations elicited by them. It necessarily had led to this split and the corresponding cessation of the tension. The laws could not apply to reason or to the self; that is why the sphere of the mind had to be separated from somatic psychology. On the other hand, this separation was the prerequisite to the emergence of psychology. For science has to account for all the phenomena within its scope, or at least has to have at its disposal the means required to yield a satisfactory explanation. Without the separation, this could not have been brought to pass. It was necessary, then, to place the unexplainable outside the domain of the newly created science. This is the inner logic of the situation that fostered modern psychology. This process is a typical and frequent form of the development of the sciences.

Windelband, Cassirer, and Alexander demonstrated that in vain did Descartes separate the two worlds, for the tension had left its mark on his philosophy. Both the world of pure reason and the world of experience possess inconsistencies in his system. I have not the space here to point out these inconsistencies, but it has to be emphasized that the new psychology regards as its aim the surmounting of the difficulties presented by that tension and the inclusion of all psychic phenomena under a unified system of laws (Köhler [31]; Lewin: *Vorsatz, Wille und Bedürfnis, Einleitung*; E. Straus: *Vom Sinn der Sinne*). Evidently their violent opposition to Descartes was occasioned by this orientation.

We would be lacking a certain sense of history did we not indicate the historical necessity of Descartes' position. With his sharp dualism Descartes created a climate that favored the accumulation of the information needed to solve the problems of knowledge and psychology.

In Descartes' system, then, the problem of associations played a part in establishing the relationship between mind and body and in determining the nature of ideas and the epistemological foundation of rationalistic idealism. At the same time it became the first foundation of modern psychology as well.

Hobbes: The Origins of
Mechanistic Psychology

IN THE HISTORY of the concept of associations the chain
of ideas led from Descartes through the occasionalists
to Spinoza. Descartes' own ideas gain in depth as we
follow their course. Yet the main branch of the development of the concept of association grew in a different
direction.

I

Along the main line of development of the concept of
association, Descartes was succeeded by his contemporary, Hobbes. Hobbes did not pluck his theory only from
the main branch of the history of association, but also
from fresh shoots of Renaissance parentage. From Bacon
the road to the British empiricists leads through Hobbes.
Cartesian doctrine was united with Hobbes' in the teach-
ings of the English empiricists. We shall see that Hobbes,
although he adopted the program of his master, Bacon,
evolved a theory of associations that was independent of
the latter's efforts in the same field. We shall repeatedly
encounter such turns in the course of our study. Views,
maxims, examples of associative relationships—all these

may be adopted, yet the motivation for the attitude the individual assumes regarding associations is hidden in the innermost recesses of the philosopher's personality. It is an integral part thereof founded on personal experience and incapable of being philosophically further analyzed.

As regards associations, Hobbes followed the path of Fracastoro (7) and, more significantly, Telesio (8), whose doctrines rather approximated sensualism. These philosophers interpreted their own inner experiences with a facility conceivable only in the Renaissance man who had just shed the leveling spectacles of scholasticism. They seized upon their own experiences and their observations of their own processes of thinking and tried to formulate a science out of them. The points of departure of scholasticism were distant, thus scholastic doctrine contemplated personal everyday experiences in the light of general metaphysical principles. But during the Renaissance personal experience became the starting point. Thus was association, our most common everyday experience, brought into focus.

Fracastoro posed the problem of the formation of concepts. "How does the notion of generality develop from singular sense perceptions which we possess, and how does it become a universal concept?" he asked (7). He replied by introducing the idea of the subnotio. According to him the subnotio is the capacity of the mind to break up the contents of experience into its elements. The subnotio is not a judgement, nor is it purely sense perception; it is an instinctive bridge between cognitive contents. In this sense, all the functions of the human mind become a process of synthesizing and analyzing. This is but a loose and undogmatic concept of association.

This groping still retains a glimpse of the entirety of personal experience, of consciously or unconsciously pigeonholing new impressions with the nearest thought and concept, or of trying to find a more intimate contact between two thus-connected experiences. Every philosopher may recognize his own first youthful intimations in the thoughts of the eminent representatives of this second childhood of Western philosophy.

This train of thought culminates in Fracastoro's belief that the concept is a "similarity" between groups of experiences. According to him this similarity cannot be thought to have independent objective existence, even though it does exist independently of the observer. This empirical approach, practically untouched by speculation, is a suitable point of departure for further investigation, but it contains the danger of mechanization in its simplifying tendency. Indeed, Hobbes was unable to avoid it. In this form empiricism is not yet a science; although in the following statement, Kantian transcendental deduction and the spiritual climate of a priori experiential functions are discernible: "In the first appearance of the empirical content, the subnotio is already present. Without the capacity of dividing, without gradual apperception and the analysis of each component of a complexum not even the beginnings of a concept could be formed" (7).

The same thoughts were expressed by Telesio, but in a more general, and at once more mechanized, form. He combined them with the notion of physiological memory traces, already known to us from Descartes. Here we encounter only the first traces of mechanization. It is worthy of note that mechanization began with these Renaissance naturalists and that it was gradually more accentuated with the development of the natural sciences.

This phenomenon is a tempting target for the comparative study of science to examine the reciprocal actions between the sciences and the scientific panorama of different periods. In our day, with structural changes in the development of the natural sciences, corresponding structural modifications in psychology are discernible. There is a trend away from mechanistic conceptions and toward dynamic interpretations.

For Telesio intelligence is the manifold application of physiological memory. This indicates that he regards associations found in experience as the foundation of the mode of functioning of the intelligence, as can be seen from the following quotations:

> All understanding we can obtain about the nature of things is founded on the ability to recognize similar impressions as such, and that from the immediately given parts of complexes we can go to the whole complex in which we previously encountered it. . . . In this way, from certain known qualities of a body— hardness, pliability, color—we arrive directly to the empirical whole we designate with the term and concept of "gold." . . . Our entire life and intellection goes back to such analogical suppositions [8].

Judging from these quotations, Telesio regards intelligence as one of the senses, namely, the sense that perceives objects not present. Thus he conceives of intelligence not as a judging power over the senses but as one of them. This is the foundation of his sensualism, which is an epistemology founded wholly on sense perceptions, even though for him the first datum and point of departure is given by objects.

II

Regarding the cognitive process and the nature of the psychical, Hobbes received his inspiration from these two philosophers. From Bacon he learned that real knowledge is knowledge of the causes of things ([1] II, p. 144). To clarify the issue of this twofold inheritance in Hobbes' work, we have to examine two characteristics of his age which influenced him decisively.

The progress of the natural sciences and the discovery of natural laws in the sense of mechanics was perhaps never as promising as in Hobbes' time. The men of that age must have been struck by the possibility that the application of the laws of mechanics could explain their accustomed everyday yet fundamentally mysterious surroundings. Phenomena that had up to then been attributed to providence or chance, miracles that could be interpreted only as the intervention of supernatural forces suddenly became self-evident when mechanical laws were applied to them. It was at least conceivable that for phenomena until then utterly unaccountable some kind of explanation could be found. And this possibility amounted to breaking the fetters of the mind; for there are no greater fetters than those of helpless, perplexed inconceivability. Thus Hobbes, with Bacon's heritage in hand (the knowledge of causes is the only true knowledge), searched for necessary causality even in psychic phenomena. The possibility was shown in the example of mechanics, the tools were provided by the theory of association of these three Renaissance philosophers. What distinguished Hobbes from them was that for him only insight into causes could render empiricism a science. In his conception, the theories of these philosophers are attached to one another by the uniformity of mechanical laws, and cease to be merely the data of personal experience. Hobbes related the thoughts of Renaissance philosophers to mechanical notions, so he was obliged to separate associations into ordered and unordered ones, thereby splitting psychic life into two parts, as did Descartes. Ordered associations and their mechanical sequences become the basic law of thinking, while the unordered ones are completely ignored.

It was hoped that mechanics would explain these experiences if an event, such as thinking, taking place in the body were regarded as motion. Hobbes observed the changing nature and appearance of sensations and concluded that these changes correspond to various states of the body ([23] p. 161). And, as he showed that in bodies change is possible only by motion, he could assert:

Sense, therefore, is some internal motion in the sentient generated by some internal motion of the parts of the object and propagated through all the media to the innermost part of the organ. For the motion of any continued body one part follows another by cohesion [(23) 116, 123].

. . . so we have no transition from one imagination to another, whereof we have never had the like before in our senses. The reason whereof is this. All fancies are motions within us, relics of those made in the sense; and those motions that immediately succeeded one another in the sense, continue also together after sense: insomuch as the former coming again to take place, and be predominant, the latter followeth, by coherence of the matter moved [(24) I, 3].

This, then is Hobbes' mechanical psychology; as we shall see it does not embrace the entire domain of psychic life.

III

The other decisive influence on the philosophy of Hobbes was the changing course of the English civil wars, which often perturbed the peace of the philosopher and even obliged him to leave his homeland. Through his awakened interest in sociology, this left its mark upon his entire philosophy. I have to point out here that Hobbes' view—*earum tantum rerum scientia per demonstrationem illam a priore hominibus concessa est, quarum generatio dependet ab ipsorum hominum arbitrio* (*De Homine*, Chap. X, 4)—stems not only from the recognition of the experimental requirements of the natural sciences, which he inherited from Bacon, but is above all the product of his sociological convictions. For this requirement is not a necessary concomitant of Hobbes' geometric natural science, but only a consequence of his sociological views.

Amidst the horrors and chaos of civil war, the question permanently looming over the social scene was: What action and what arrangement truly serves the interests of the community? But the complex of possible actions is just as manifold as the complex of associations presenting themselves in connection with objects. The right action, to be chosen from among a multitude of possibilities, and the correct opinion, to be picked from the complex of associations, pose the same problem. We can understand only by virtue of the identical nature of the problems involved that Hobbes viewed as valid science only that which pertains to something that can be brought about by human volition. Hobbes, then, wanted to choose action as the criterion. From this angle we can understand his view about the contractual nature of human society and the artificial origin of language.

The civil war must have made a very deep impression on him. He must have seen that man can rule over only that which he himself had created—and not always even that. While for the naturalists only that which came into existence was logically perceptible, for Hobbes only that which was brought about by man fell into that category. The first point of departure of the object coming into existence is still in the realm of possibility and not of necessity; it is in the realm of the empirical and of free associations, and not in the sphere of closed geometrical relationships. As regards this aspect, Cassirer (1) summarized Hobbes' view as follows: "Hobbes deduces the real political power relationships from the originally free volitional activity of the individual. . . . The product of intelligence is once for all separated from the conditions of its creation, it becomes absolute reality, surrounds us with inexorable necessity and prescribes for us the laws of thinking and of action." The truth of this thesis has often been proved by history. This is the philosophical fable of the *Zauberlehrling: "Die ich rief, die Geister, werd ich nun nicht los."* It seems probable that such experiences convinced Hobbes that the welfare of society would be secured better by a firm-willed prince than by the chaos-brewing dynamism of social relationships. He sided with mechanics against dynamism. His point of view shut out the "unordered" part of associations from psychology by its own inner logic, in order to create the uniformity of mental life in associational mechanism, just as he could imagine the welfare of society only through a centrally guided and carefully surveyed mechanism. His view of the natural sciences is analogous, being essentially a geometry and barely cognizant of dynamics. But his geometry is also analogous; its definitions are not derived from the actual genesis of solids but are limited to their laws of construction. (The sphere arises by rotating a circle about its diameter.)

IV

We have delineated the twofold effect of these historical influences in the genesis of mechanistic psychology. Now our task is to shed light upon certain details of the mechanistic conception and to indicate the beginnings of sensualism.

According to Hobbes motions starting out from objects affect the body.

> . . . from the reaction . . . a phantasm or idea hath its being; which, by reason that the endeavor is now outwards, doth always appear as something situate without the organ. . . . For a phantasm is the act of sense . . . [(23) p. 117].

> For he that perceives that he hath perceived, remembers" [(23) p. 115].

Evidently for Hobbes immediate reality consists of sensations alone. We know objects through them—even the memory is a sense, although it is a prerequisite to all mental activity. (The same idea recurs in Kant.) But if remembering is a sense activity, that is, if mental processes have their basis in sensations, then association (which up to this point had been considered to be merely the mechanism of acts of sense perception and phantasm) becomes the mechanism of all mental function.

At this point Hobbes was still in a position to regard sensations as true external realities, after the fashion of the two abovementioned naturalists. In that case direct sensations and their associative connections would represent links with the external world (as they are later in Spinoza). But Hobbes' mechanistic ideal of logic requires an unequivocal uniformity and law which cannot be exposed to the hazards of empiricism. For that reason associative mechanisms later take the place of the self-developing inner dynamism of empiricism. These mechanisms ensure the unequivocal uniformity of psychic phenomena and causality: truth is the absence of contradiction of the sensations and not of the external world—this is the sensualism of Hobbes. The associative mechanism of thinking receives the following treatment in his doctrine:

> This train of thought, or mental discourse, is of two sorts. The first is unguided, without design, and inconstant . . . in which case the thoughts are said to wander, and seem impertinent to one another, as in a dream.
>
> The second is more constant; as being regulated by some desire, and design . . . From desire arises the thought of some means we have seen produce the like of that which we aim at; and from the thought of that, the thought of means to that mean; and so continually, till we come to some beginning within our own power. And because the end, by the greatness of the impression, comes often to mind, in case our thoughts begin

to wander, they are quickly again reduced into the way . . . that is to say, in all your actions, look often upon what you would have, as the thing that directs all your thoughts in the way to attain it.

The train of regulated thoughts is of two kinds: one, when of an effect imagined we seek the causes, or means that produce it; and this is common to man and beast. The other is, when imagining anything whatsoever, we seek all the possible effects that can by it be produced . . . Of which I have not at any time seen any sign but in man only . . . [(24) III].

This indicates that Hobbes also recognized unregulated associations that do not occur mechanically. But he was not interested in their source—he ascribed them to lack of purposiveness and considered them undeserving of investigation. By thus disposing of unordered associations, he arrived at his sensualism, at the unequivocality of sensations; thus was his mechanistic philosophy born. The only way he could dispose of unregulated associations was by disregarding them. Unable to perceive their importance, he conceived of human existence in a mechanistic, nominalistic way, never arriving at the dynamics of being. Here we see a return of the conception of the Aristotelian crystal spheres into psychology. Well-known modern psychologists, among them Lewin and Köhler, maintain that this was due to a lack of trust in the free development of man. Accordingly, we find no reference to the unconscious in Hobbes. Windelband ([5] p. 155) points out that Hobbes spoke of two psychic systems. We have treated of the theoretical system here. This starts out from sensations; its mode of functioning is characterized by associations, culminating in the power to calculate. Hobbes goes so far as to assert that all intellectual activity can be reduced to addition and subtraction. That way he flattens Telesio's deep conception of composition and decomposition into mathematical formulas. Hobbes' practical system comprises volitional activities, which move between the basic antipodes of attraction and repulsion. This practical system is subjected to the theoretical—so much so that in one place Hobbes declared that will and judgment are one and the same ([23] 176). The analogy between Kant's theory and these systems is remarkable. Thus there is a trace of a dynamism of impulses in Hobbes, of an instinctual channeling of associations; but the intellectual mechanism rules over that too.

This will suffice to show how Hobbes became the point of departure for a mechanistic psychology of associations that tried to evade the problems. Since the practical system is subjected to the theoretical, there could be no mention in associational psychology of the unconscious or of the independent development of instinctual phenomena. At the same time it is evident that the purposive quality of associations in Hobbes is still very far from similar tendencies manifested in modern psychology (Ach: *determinierende Tendenz*; Lewin: *Taetigkeitsbereitschaft*). The significance of this purpose is here altogether intellectual and conscious and is used merely to explain the mechanism of association.

V

Hobbes did not solve the problem of association. He does not sharply go out against it as Descartes did, nor does he embrace it with the eagerness of Spinoza. He evades the core of the problem, and consequently his psychology becomes superficial and destitute of inner connections. Like Descartes, he made no attempt to unify the whole of psychic life under a single law. But, again like Descartes, he was thereby obliged to disregard a significant portion of mental phenomena. Descartes excludes the highest faculties of judgment and thinking from psychology; Hobbes excludes the most interwoven, complicated, seemingly meaningless regions of psychic life—those bordering on the instinctual and unconscious. Yet it has to be said for the sake of a complete understanding of Hobbes' philosophy that the sociological aspect of his thinking may have made this exclusion necessary.

In judging social questions in Hobbes' age, the mechanism of human cognitive processes had to be decisive. The emancipation of the product of reason and its seeming independence of deeper interrelations appeared certain. By evading the examination of deeper psychic relationships, Hobbes created a suitable climate for an examination of the effects produced by such cognitive processes. In the midst of civil war, the effect of the struggle of ideologies on the fate of the groups partaking in that struggle constituted the central problem. The psychological genesis of these ideologies—the emotive, instinctive causes of the identification of the individual with one or the other of them—will necessarily suffer neglect in favor of political problems. We do not have to suppose a conscious evasion on Hobbes' part; it is more likely that the searching mind and the inner economy of attention produce such partial superficialities. Hobbes created the science of the conscious superstratum of psychic life with his associative mechanics and with his sensualistic-nominalistic doctrine.

Spinoza: Toward a Psychological Analysis of Mysticism

I

THE TASK, replete as it is with contradictions, of assimilating, reconciling and developing the heritage of Descartes and Hobbes, fell to Spinoza. Descartes attributed the free play of associations, which can recall the images of external objects and occasion thought without the actual presence of causes, to the influence of the body. This view gave rise to radical epistemological consequences. This made him separate the body, giving rise to muddled concepts, from pure reason; thereby he created the first great dualistic system of modern philosophy. This led him almost to the brink of skepticism by the methodology of *de omnibus dubitandum*. This caused him to find in the *"ideae innatae"* the only source of knowledge and thence his rationalistic system.

Descartes, possessed of doubt and motivated by skepticism, searched for and found in the ego and in the innate ideas the rock of certainty; for Spinoza this certainty was already given. God, the intellectual love of God, the indivisible unity of God and the world: these were his most profound inner experiences, which Cassirer, Windelband,

and Alexander alike call a mystical experience. He preserved these intact all his life; they, in turn, saved him
from skepticism.

Hobbes, despairing of the harmony of extramental
objects, wished to grasp being by a gradual realization of
the harmony of sensations or sense perceptions (sensualism) and designations (nominalism); for Spinoza existence is a priori given in God and the meaning of existence
a priori given in the unity of God and the world.

II

At the same time Spinoza was well aware of the fact of
associations. The security provided by his solid starting
point let him penetrate their nature to a depth previously
unattained.

In the *Theologico-Political Treatise* we read: "So too
the law that man in remembering one thing straightway
remembers another either like it or which is perceived
simultaneously with it, is a law which necessarily follows
from the nature of man" (Section 61). Spinoza cites this
instance as an example of natural law, as opposed to
laws of society. But subsequent passages indicate that already in this work the significance of the proposition far
surpasses the significance of the example used. Actually
Spinoza pointed out here that, since the social law depends on man's will (this is Hobbes' heritage) and man
himself is part of nature, social laws are necessarily derived from the natural law. Then he adds—and this is the
momentous point for us—"I have stated that these laws
depend on human decree, because it is well to define and
explain things by their proximate causes. The general
consideration of fate and the concatenation of causes

would aid us very little in forming and arranging our ideas concerning particular questions." And in the *Short Treatise* he unmistakably states the relationship of law and will: ". . . all laws which cannot be transgressed are divine laws, for the reason that all that happens is not contrary to but consequence of God's own decree" ([25], 101).

Thus, *sub specie determinatis*, all human thought, all covenants are lawful, but one has to search for the proximate determining cause. Accordingly Spinoza, even though he was aware of the role of associations, still thought that everything human or natural was lawful. He was not led astray by the apparent chaos of associations. The divine nature of the universe was always evident for him. This helped him to extend the causal theory of modern thought which he had inherited from Bruno and Hobbes to the entire universe, including psychic phenomena, where even Descartes—one of the founders of modern thinking—had failed.

Yet these quotations have more than a merely epistemological significance. Because it is probable that Spinoza considered causality (the proximate cause) as one of the associations (the eternal destiny of things). This connection is rendered more probable also by the chapter in *On the Improvement of Understanding* devoted to fictions: "There are some who doubt of true ideas through not having attended to the distinction between a true perception and all others. . . . I shall not here give the *essence of every perception* and explain it through its *proximate cause*. Such work lies in the province of philosophy. I shall confine myself to what concerns method, that is to the character of fictions, false and doubtful perceptions. . . ."

Thus he contrasted the proximate cause with the fictions; but the fictions, as we will presently show, are themselves occasioned by associations. From among all associations one stands out in particular: the proximate cause. Spinoza later asserted ([26] 36) that "the inadequate and chaotic ideas follow with the same necessity as the adequate ones." This is why the eternal destiny of things—as contrasted to the most proximate cause—and the role of fictions are analogous. The difference between the two—and we will return to this point—can be discerned in the incompleteness of the latter.

In the conclusion of this train of thought Spinoza pointed out that the fiction concerns only possible things —not necessary ones, whose nonexistence implies a contradiction, nor impossible ones, whose very existence implies that contradiction. He wrote: "No fiction creates anything new in the mind; they only recall into the memory that which is already present in the brain and the imagination. At such times the mind concentrates its attention on every thing at once, but in a chaotic fashion. If for instance we summon into the memory a speech and a tree at the same time, and the mind, without discriminating between them, is concentrated on both at once, we think that the tree speaks." He then pointed out that the fiction may refer to three things (and *here* is the deficiency!): to the existence, reality, and essence of objects.

But what is fiction contrasted to the "proximate cause"? Possibility contrasted to necessity and impossibility? The chaotic idea recalled to the mind without the creation of anything new? What is the quoted connection of speech to tree if not associations? This culminates in the— mostly falsely interpreted—thesis of *omnis determinatio*

—*negatio*. This is but a renewed expounding of Spinoza's demand: "true ideas must be separated from the rest" (*On the Improvement of Understanding*, 22). And the singling out and upholding of one association apparently means the denial of all others.

As for fictions regarding the existence, reality, and essence of objects, they are those same various aspects of association which we met in Descartes and which assume central importance in Hume and Kant. There is a profound observation in this threefold grouping. For Spinoza saw that the existence of objects—the English school limited this to coexistence and succession—just as their essence, falls into the domain of the meeting and associative joining of things. The same applies to the reality of objects, which is nothing but the appearance of objects on different levels of human consciousness.

Spinoza's analysis of fiction ends with the following:

. . . further, as a fictitious idea cannot be distinct, but is necessarily confused . . . the mind has only partial knowledge of a thing either simple or complex and does not distinguish between the known and the unknown, and again it directs its attention promiscuously to all parts of an object at once, without making distinctions, it follows, *first* that the idea be of something very simple, it must necessarily be clear and distinct. For a very simple object cannot be known in part, it must either be known altogether or not at all. *Secondly,* it follows that if a complex object be divided by thought into a number of simple component parts, and if each part be regarded separately, all confusion will disappear. *Thirdly,* it follows that fiction cannot be simple, but is made up of the blending of several confused ideas of diverse objects . . . [*On the Improvement of the Understanding*, pp. 23–24].

With this we have returned to the starting point. The most clearly perceptible is always the unassociated, the noncompound, the simple, the final—the a priori idea of the divinity. Everything else has to be analyzed in its parts in order to be understood. In the last analysis, it has to be traced back to God, the source of all knowing. In analyzing the cognitive process, Spinoza expounded on this further and in a clearer fashion.

We have seen in the foregoing that, in his knowledge of associations, and despite the apparent chaos they manifest, Spinoza firmly resisted all doubt and was convinced of the possibility of understanding. We will now review the method of this cognition.

III

Cognition according to Spinoza derives from two sources. The first, which remained unchanged throughout his philosophical career, may best be summarized by his own definitions in the *Ethics*:

1. By that which is self-caused, I mean that of which the essence involves existence, or that of which the nature is only conceivable as existent.

2. By substance, I mean that which is in itself, and is conceived through itself: in other words, that of which a conception can be formed independently of any other conception.

These two definitions are clear enough. The substance, the divinity, is its own cause. It is not accompanied by associative concepts, one of which would be the cause. One does not have to choose between possibilities, between real and fictitious causes. This is the firm point in reference to which everything can be assigned its proper meaning and measure.

The other basic source was subject to a great metamorphosis in the course of the development of Spinoza's thought and remained constant only where it concerned the first source. This second source may be characterized as follows. Since thinking is a divine attribute, He "has to possess about every really existent thing, substance, or modus without exception a concept, a mode of thought, an understanding" ([26"] 42).

While the quotation taken from the *Theologico-Political Treatise* taught only that associations comprised the mechanism of psychic life, these latter quotes served as a foundation of the cognitive process—partly by pointing out that the idea of the divinity is the unchangeable condition of the genesis of these relationships and partly by showing that the thus-established mechanism embraces the entire world of being. Thus thinking is based on the idea of the divinity which is incapable of being further analyzed; its mode of functioning is association, and the whole world is reflected in it.

In the *Short Treatise* Spinoza explains in greater detail the psychological foundations of knowing.

Now because the body is the first thing of which our soul becomes aware, and because, as had been said, the idea which the thinking subject has of each thing that exists in nature is the soul of that thing, the thing must then necessarily be the first cause of that idea [(25) 98].

Now the reason why one person is more conscious of his truth than another, is that the idea of affirmation (or denial) corresponds entirely with the nature of the thing and therefore has more essence [(25) 74].

Desire stems also from experience, as is seen in the practice of physicians who are accustomed to look upon a certain remedy as an infallible one if they have found it to be good in a few instances [(25) 51].

Experience-generated desires encapsulate an association, a method of thinking. Basically, Spinoza refers here to the drive-directed nature of the associational process.

At the same time, these views show Spinoza's relationship to empiricism. For these theses have a decisive import as regards sensualistic and empirical psychology and epistemology. Hobbes was prompted by similar considerations to create his associational mechanics. But in Spinoza, the significance of these theses is fundamentally different if we examine them in the light of the data of the source of knowledge.

Namely, there are three kinds of knowing: one based on opinion, one on faith, and one on love. The first corresponds to the empirical: by it, we know the essence of being; the second to inference: by it, we know objects through their effects; the third to intuition: by it, we know existence through its causes. "The first is opinion, since empirical knowledge is subject to error." (Spinoza regards the perception of empirical objects as associative connections which may be partial and thus mistaken.) "The second is faith, for objects of which we are aware only through our reason are not present to us and consequently we know only logically and through conviction that they are such and not otherwise." (In another passage Spinoza expresses this as follows: "It only shows what an object should be, not what it really is." By this he implicitly passes judgment on rationalism. It appears clear that he attributes a regularity proper to reason, the law of "it has to be," which he demonstrates in the *Ethics* to be an associative law too.) "The third: love. It is pure understanding which does not take place merely through a process of logical conviction but through emotion and the enjoyment of the object: it is the first one among all kinds of knowledge!" ([25] 47). We see a certain contradiction between Sections 98 and 47 of the *Short Treatise*. While according to Section 98 the soul is constituted of experience, Section 47 affirms that this experiential knowledge is subject to chance and error. We can conclude that Spinoza had not yet eliminated the inconsistency that had presented itself in Descartes. This confusion, a Cartesian inheritance, looms over the cradle of Spinoza's system. On the other hand, we can also perceive Hobbes' mechanism there ([25] 98). Empiricism, rationalism, and mysticism blended at this stage of Spinoza's development and together created cognition. With this synthesis of epistemologies, Spinoza long preceded Kant. We have seen the fixed point by the aid of which Spinoza produced this synthesis. But we have yet to explain the *how* of that process.

IV

. . . when we use our understanding aright in the cognition of things, we must know them in their causes.

Now, then, since God is a first cause of all other things, the knowledge of God according to the nature of things (*ex rerum natura*) must precede the knowledge of the first cause. True love always springs from the knowledge that its object is glorious and good . . . it can be poured out more ardently upon no one than the Lord, our God . . . [(25) 58, 76].

In contrast to this "Hate is the inclination to ward off from ourselves something which has done us harm" ([25] 58, 78). Hatred and its degrees keep things apart from man; they may even annihilate them. That is, they do just the opposite of the work of love; they prevent understanding. But since the understanding of the world means the understanding of God, and thus the attainment of perfection, ". . . if we use our reason aright we can have no hate, nor aversion toward anything, because by so doing we would deprive ourselves of the perfection which inheres in everything" ([25] 58).

This thought will become really understandable only if we compare it with certain passages of the *Ethics*:

All ideas, insofar as they are referred to God, are true [(26) II, 32].

There is nothing positive in ideas which causes them to be called false [(26) II, 33].

Every idea which in us is absolute or adequate or perfect is true [(26) II, 34].

Falsity consists in the privation of knowledge, which inadequate, fragmentary, or confused ideas involve [(26) II, 35].

Inadequate and confused ideas follow by the same necessity as adequate or clear and distinct ideas [(26) II, 36].

Thus, knowledge of the real order of the world of objects leads us to God. In Him every concept has its cause. That is, every concept is true; only incomplete, inadequate ones can be false, because they make the impression of being complete; the progressive cognition of concepts eliminates the imperfections and thus leads to the knowledge of God. Thus, in the unified regularity of the world of being every association necessarily has its own cause, and it is misleading only when we do not refer it to the whole but accept it as whole as we receive it. Consequently, the right method assigns *its own place to everything.* In Spinoza's words, "the right method cannot consist in that after we have obtained the ideas [obviously in an intuitive manner] . . . we should still search for the notes of reality, but rather in the way in which we find truth itself; that is, we find the existence of things or ideas (because these designate the same) *in the proper order.*" We can achieve this order by tracing each association, each emerging possibility back to its own sources and connect it with its own roots. The key to knowing is thus the act of opening up for each concept: love, the disarming of hate, the path of understanding everything. This all-embracing concept then unites the first two ways of knowing in the third. By this, Spinoza dissolved the problem of knowing in a huge network of associations. As contrasted to empiricism and reason, which tried to tame the wild play of associations with a variety of means, Spinoza entrusted man and his science to intuition and consequently to associations, which are the

most deeply hidden resources of the human mind, thereby
subordinating to them the other two sources of knowledge. This step shows a certain kinship with Descartes'
turning to the self. The concept of the self performs the
same role in the Cartesian system as the notion of God
does in Spinoza's doctrine. "God does not talk to men with
words." Reason is so fused with God that He knows it
immediately, through intuition. In this we can perceive
a Heraclitean echo: "The prince whose seat is at Delphi
does not speak or keep secrets, he gives signs." Reason,
then, knows God through intuition whence it has to infer
the reality of existence deductively. But before treating
this, we will have to devote some discussion to this latter
"pure" form of knowledge—intuition.

V

Love is the source of knowledge, intuition, and opening up; true knowledge is given in fusion with the universe. These are all very ancient beliefs; they were the
cornerstone of every kind of mysticism, including Bud-
dhist mysticism. It would lead us far afield to analyze
here the essence of mysticism. We will confine ourselves
to a few remarks only. We have seen that Spinoza urges
us to struggle against the selecting activity ingrained in
human nature: let us lay ourselves open before everything and let reality permeate us unaffected by the influence of passions. This demand is carried of course much
farther in mysticism. Yoga practices, the three degrees of
ecstasy in Buddhism, the fasts and self-torments of the
cabalists—all these conquered enormous cravings, desires, and instinctive energies so that they should not
govern thinking, "in order that man may see things in

their essence." Thus, they wanted to annihilate the force that would channel the series of association in definite directions. Their aim was to arrive at the understanding of the divinity, the wholeness of the universe, freeing themselves from all barriers. Spinoza's demand—which sought to eliminate hatred so that the self may be united (this is the word he uses in the *Short Treatise*) with the real order without discrimination—is analogous to it.

This was the inner purpose that he never actually achieved. These deep-searching theses are aspirations rather than thoughts. They are only the axis around which Spinoza turned Hobbes' problem in order to subject the logical order to a unified regularity—after the order of tangible reality had already been reduced to such a regularity by Hobbes. Yet the system Spinoza built around that axis is rife with contradictions; for its core remains but a turning point and is not realized.

VI

On the Improvement of Understanding shows the decisive turning point in Spinoza's development. Here we can still find the problem of the influence of confusion-begetting associations. Cassirer sums this up: "Every satisfaction becomes the immediate source of a new desire. We are constantly chased from one object to another" ([1] II, p. 11). At the same time the opposite side is already discernible, the final evolution of Spinoza's thought: "Only an eternal and unending existence could supply a firm basis and safety to the mind." The former expresses the constant associative progression from concept to concept, which hinders true knowledge. The latter is the *"sub specie aeternitatis"* perspective, in which all associations constitute the adequate concepts of the *correspond-ing events in the real world*. For persons lost in the labyrinth and regarding every turn as contingent, Spinoza suggests a vantage point whence to survey the entire labyrinth at a glance. This dual viewpoint shows the direction of Spinoza's development. As observed from inside the labyrinth, associations make for confusion in that restricted circle; but in the unified view of the laby-rinth, *sub specie aeternitatis*, they come to be invested with regularity. By this means he ensures the continuity of associations in conformity with the natural law. The possible thought connections exist also in the real order. Today we would say: even if a thought appeared mean-ingless or misleading at first glance, as regards the human mind and the entire world of reality, the relationship to which its existence can be attributed will always be found.

VII

It is along this line that *On the Improvement of Under-standing* turned against the empiricism of the *Short Treatise*. "We know that the operations producing the images obey laws completely different from the rational law." But, as Cassirer ([1] II, p. 16) noted, Spinoza also maintained that reason and cause are one and the same. The shift from one thesis to the other clearly indicates the path of Spinoza's development. While according to the empirical view associations play a disturbing role and clash with the laws of thinking and inference—as in the case of morals, reason and self-seeking interests conflict with the intuitively felt "good"—in the new perspective this opposition ceased. Here Spinoza accepted every effect as regular, since he regarded everything alike as divine and uniform. There are, as it were, no more influences: what happens in the soul happens in the extended world. The effort, aimed at bringing psychic phenomena under a unified rule, led to the complete abandonment of psychic laws. The independent existence of psychic laws has ended: reason and cause coincided. It is like the story about the man who wished to furnish his museum so as to make it as much like nature as possible and yet to have it contain everything. Nature itself became the museum. If one is wise one must see that the right solution is to enjoy nature itself; but then the idea of the museum is lost. Spinoza realized this. Whence comes the doctrine of *ordo et connexio rerum, idem est vel ordo et connexio idearum*—an axiom imbued with the force of revelation. Yet he could not give up the principle of the museum. The reason for this is not to be sought in Spinoza's will. It happened as a natural consequence of the inner dialectics of his thoughts. The search for regularity and the rescuing of these from the influence of associations prompted him to discern the general regularities. And this he could achieve only by "rising above the labyrinth" —that is, by intuition. Of course, this did not change the original program, the deductive synthetic method. On the contrary, it was its climax. Spinoza had to infer everything deductively from the divine substance. This is the origin of the geometric form of the *Ethics* as a final victory over skepticism and the unambiguous and demonstrable formula of necessary connections.

VIII

Spinoza deduced the manifestations of being from substance by means of the attributes and modes. The contradictions pointed out above are most clearly expressed in the doctrine of the attribute. For that reason we have to examine that doctrine more closely.

"Every substance is necessarily infinite" ([26] 8). "The more reality or being a thing has, the greater the number of its attributes" ([26] 9). "God, or substance, consisting of infinite attributes, of which each expresses eternal and infinite essentiality, necessarily exists" ([26] 11).

Later Spinoza acquiesces in the fact that only two of this infinity of man's attributes—thinking and extension —can be known to man ([26] Propositions I, II; /5/ p. 20). But if being can be understood deductively from substance, and divine substance has an infinite number of attributes, why is it that only two of man's attributes can be known? The reason is apparent: the system is a construct—the two attributes did not come to be known to him deductively a priori but empirically a posteriori. Spinoza did not draw conclusions about the attributes from a priori substances; rather these were already given empirically, just as the concept of God is given by intuition. And as regards associations, Spinoza was aware that things have an infinity of relations and that consequently an infinity of associational connections may develop among them. But he designated as knowable the spatial and cognitive relationships. This choice was suggested to him by Descartes. Later, associational psychology repeated this choice in the form of coexistence and succession ([1] pp. 36–38). Cassirer expounded a similar view. After making this choice the plan at the point of departure remained naturally unaccomplished; the huge pantheistic program which we described as mystical was not fulfilled.

IX

The interpretation we gave to the inner dynamism of Spinoza's thought is supported by the difficulty presented to Spinoza by the concepts formed of other concepts and of the mind. For, as every concept has referents in the extended world, it may be asked what corresponds to the concept of the mind, to the concept of that concept, and so forth, in the extended world. Windelband ([5] p. 228) observed that there are hints of a solution in Spinoza's correspondence. According to this Spinoza "supposed such a relationship of attributes by which, because of their succession, the modes of the preceding attributes would also be the modes of the succeeding one. Thus, all attributes would be founded on the attributes of extension." This means that the layers of conceptual strata—an infinite number of them—thus produced, would be the rest of the attributes, and their hierarchy would yield the understanding of all relationships of objects. Thus the notion of adequate order, which we have dealt with before, acquires a new meaning because the adequate arrangement in the orders of reality (*subsumptio*) becomes a necessary prerequisite of understanding. These orders of reality, the reflection of things in the human mind, and the further reflection of this reflection—as in a room with opposite walls covered with mirrors—have a double significance: the contact of thoughts and of the thinking of thoughts mean associations, and they re-illumine the problems of knowledge presented by the emergence of the "adequate order."

The question of *orders of reality* recur in Hume and Kant. Throughout the history of philosophy, the fact that the real order has greatly varied reflections in consciousness has been prominent. The variety of these reflections and their interconnection indicate in Spinoza's system that no mechanism can solve the problems of psychology. In modern psychology the problems presented by the levels of consciousness—that is to say, these orders of reality—lead beyond the psychophysical theory of associations.

It will be understood, then, why Spinoza could not develop the theory of the knowability of the other attributes. This would have realized the original mystic-pantheistic program—had he, accordingly, given up the privileged position of the attributes of extension and thinking. He then would have had to give up empiricism, which was a fundamental factor for him, together with its relation to geometry and the modern natural sciences. The attempt mentioned above, treated by Windelband, also secured the special position of the attribute of extension, even if at the price of a certain concession.

Spinoza was thus prompted by associations and by mysticism to create his specific pantheistic formula—and that in the form of mysticism. In his system, body and soul, matter and spirit, are equally divine attributes. Consequently, they are governed by the same laws. Reason and cause coincide. Psychology, which sharply differed from the laws of reason in Descartes, is here coincident with them. There, psychology did not cover the entire area of mental activity, because for Descartes body and spirit were split in two. For that reason, no comprehensive psychology could be created. Here, the psychic law corresponds to the law of the extended things, and consequently it cannot even achieve independent existence.

Locke: The Borderland of Sensualism and Empiricism

I

THE CONCEPT OF *associatio idearum* was created by Locke. In his *Essay* he devoted an entire chapter to it, and in another treatise, *The Conduct of Understanding*, he referred to it on several occasions. His views may be summed up in the following quotations:

> . . . there must be something that blinds their understanding, and makes them not see the falsehood of what they embrace for real truth . . . [This is the *associatio idearum*—the connection of ideas] which thus captivates their reason, and leads men of sincerity blindfolded from common sense . . . some independent ideas, of no alliance to one another, are, by education, custom, and the constant din of their party, so coupled in their minds, that they always appear there together. . . . This gives sense to jargon, demonstration to absurdities and consistency to nonsense, and is the foundation of the greatest . . . errors in the world . . . the most dangerous one, since . . . it hinders men from seeing and examining . . . fills their heads with false

*explain error by associations,
rather than by logical deduction
from incorrect premises*

Locke

views, and their reasonings with false consequences
[(9) II, 33, 18].

Some of our ideas have a natural correspondence and
connection one with another . . . There is another
connection of ideas wholly owing to *chance* and *custom* . . . and the one no sooner at any time comes into
the understanding, but its associate appears . . . [(9)
II, 33, 5]. *here, association ≠ Höffding step*

A grown person surfeiting with honey no sooner hears
the name of it, but . . . cannot bear the very idea of
it; . . . but he knows from whence . . . he got this
indisposition. Had this happened to him by an over-
dose of honey when a child, all the same effects would
have followed; but the cause would have been mistaken . . . [(9) II, 33, 7].

This is the result of the association of ideas:

Men of fair minds, and not given up to the over-ween-
ing of self-flattery, are frequently guilty of it; and in
many cases one with amazement hears the arguings,
and is astounded at the obstinacy of a worthy man,
who yields not to the evidence of reason, though laid
before him as clear as daylight. This sort of unreasonableness is usually imputed to education and prejudice,
and for the most part, truly enough, though that
reaches not to the bottom of the decease . . . I shall
be pardoned for calling it . . . madness [(9) II, 33, 2].

The phenomenon called association, as described above,
consists of several factors. The Baconian element taken

over from Descartes—that associations engender chaos—
is paramount in it. While Bacon speaks of the idols as an
attribute of the human mind, Locke describes them as
a form of mental derangement. This discrepancy springs
from two sources. Bacon's idols are connection-types.
Locke considered not types but individual examples
where concepts succeeded one another, as if compul-
sively. He designated this phenomenon as association.
He dealt with the free flight of ideas independently of
this. He did not recognize the connection between the
two. According to Locke, ideas have natural connections;
later we will examine their genesis. It is understandable,
therefore, that he regarded everything opposed to the
"natural" as a "derangement." The mechanism of association and the idea of "vital forces" were inherited from
Descartes. The concept of habit, as a force creating associations, had already occurred to Bacon and Descartes;
it was particularly stressed by Locke. It was deepened
and made more original by him and became a sovereign
part of the genetic approach to psychic phenomena.

In the *Conduct of Human Understanding* he describes
the flight of ideas after having pointed out, in Part II
Section 14 of the *Essays*, that we have to regard the mind
as a continuous succession of ideas. Here Locke notes
that it would be important to direct the flow of ideas so
that only those that actually pertain to our observations
would present themselves to the mind—and in the order
in which we have need of them. He held that whoever
would invent an instrument to render that possible would
greatly benefit mankind. Locke did not realize that the
ungovernability of the flow of associations derives from
the same source as the "pathological" phenomenon of
association. For us, the connection between them is a

proven fact. As an example he chooses the thinking of the child. He describes how children are incapable of concentrating upon one thought for any length of time. They cannot keep their minds from wandering.

The following of Locke's observations examine the mechanism of the phenomena of association and the flight of ideas:

> ... the thought ... of the mind is ... accompanied ... with pleasure or pain ... [(9) II, 20, 1].

> ... any very great and prevailing uneasiness having once laid hold on the will, let it not go; by which we may be convinced what it is that determines the will. Thus any vehement pain of the body; of the ungovernable passion of a man violently in love; or the impatient desire for revenge, keeps the will steady and intent ... never lets the understanding lay by the object, but all the thoughts of the mind and powers of the body are uninterruptedly employed that way ... It seems evident that the will ... is determined in us by an uneasiness: and whether this be not so, I desire every one to observe in himself [(9) II, 11, 39].

If we compare these passages with the characteristics attributed to associations, the inference is immediately clear: these passions, pleasure and pain, form the enormous connecting force that is in them. This is the threshold of the unconscious, especially in view of his remark on the disgust which has an unknown origin. In another place, Locke goes further and extends the scope of the dynamism of passions to the entire thinking process.

> . . . what is that determines the will in regard to our actions? And that . . . is not, as is generally supposed, the greater good in view; but some *uneasiness*. . . . This is that which successively determines the will and sets us upon those actions we perform. This uneasiness we may call as it is, *desire*; which is an uneasiness of the mind for want of some absent good [(9) II, 11, 31].

> . . . the mind [has] in most cases . . . a power to *suspend* the . . . satisfaction of any of its desires . . . to consider . . . examine . . . weigh them with others [(9) II, 11, 48].

Thus thought is the result of man's ability to postpone the fulfilment of his desires.

We have so far gained the following picture about Locke's concept of associations: Ideas are connected by habit. The force of habit is based on feelings of pleasure and pain, on the power of the passions. The ideas present in the mind are a continually rushing, leaping torrent; pleasure and pain, uneasiness, the passions propel the current. Thinking begins only when these passions can be controlled. Thinking makes the choice between these ideas in the service of our goals. The child, for instance, is not yet master of its passions; that is why it is unable to concentrate on a thought for any length of time.

From this picture the notion of Hobbes' associational mechanism is entirely lacking. A faint trace of a mechanistic conception is perhaps indicated by the role of vital forces, taken over from Descartes—but its importance is limited. This view is dominated by empirical factors held together by two basic speculative considerations. One is the dynamism of the passions, which itself starts out from experiential sources—the feeling of uneasiness, which drives us on, and the curbing of passions, which gives scope to the thinking process. (This is present in Descartes' system but in a much more rudimentary form.) The other speculative consideration is that there is a natural connection between ideas, which is disturbed by the pathological phenomenon of associations; the knowledge of this connection is called *understanding*. The examination of this natural connecting activity and of understanding is our next task.

II

According to Locke, all ideas come from sensations: "Nothing can be more certain than that the idea we gain of an external object is in our consciousness." So we see that his point of departure is sensualistic. But Locke, unlike Hobbes, did not stop at sensualism; he considered also another basic activity of the soul, reflection. In place of the anemic Hobbesian empiricism founded merely on sensation, here psychic activity is twofold: reflection absorbs the material supplied by sensation. Reflection is the proper activity of the mind: it summarizes and analyzes; in a word, it changes the sensory data. With the concept of reflection the first clearly formulated notion of mental activity proper appears in Western philosophy. Mere sensualism is transformed into empiricism. Windelband characterizes the Lockean system as "empiricism—but in the good sense of the word." The appearance of dealing with merely sensual, phenomenal material vanished. The data emerging in consciousness are molded by reflection before they are perceived. In the concept of reflection we recognize an a priori condition for the sensory data to emerge in consciousness; it is the precursor of *apprehensio, recognitio,* and *apperceptio* in Kantian transcendental deduction.

Locke's system is not devoid of sensualism; but with the aid of reflection he essays to develop sensualism in a way that would enable it to interpret the highest spiritual functions. The *simple ideas* are still the sensation of objects. Direct sensation is still the purest form of knowledge—the only one that exactly conforms to objects, the only one that is infallible.

. . . all our simple ideas are *adequate* [(9) II, 31, 2].

. . . our simple ideas are *clear*, when they are such as the objects themselves from whence they were taken did . . . present them. While the memory retains them thus . . . they are clear ideas [(9) II, 29, 2].

These are definite only when they differ from all other ideas:

. . . things ranked under distinct names are supposed different enough to be distinguished . . . what . . . makes it confused is, when it is such that it may as well be called by another name . . . and so the distinction . . . is quite lost [(9) II, 19, 6].

Simple ideas cause false knowledge only if words and names are inadequate, the impression made by the object is weak and transient, the memory is weak and cannot retain the impression as received. Thus knowledge gained through simple ideas may only be confused if associative connections (the incorrect association of names, associative changes in the memory) obscure it.

For Locke, simple ideas served as the most secure foundation for understanding, although they might lead to error. Understandably, he wanted to trace all other ideas back to them, and was led to the problem of the genesis of ideas and of psychic life. According to him, human understanding can be explained and comprehended only by the origin of our concepts. He saw the task, then, as showing how ideas are formed. Which are these simple ideas and the corresponding sensations whence the other ideas came? Does each idea have something corresponding to it in the external world? In this way, the introduction of the concept of reflection made it necessary for him to examine our ideas from the point of view of their epistemological value.

Thus it is his contention that to every idea there corresponds a simple idea and to each of these a sensation. The experiential basis of this assertion is well shown in a remark Locke made in connection with a different complex of problems to the effect that a happy notion crowned by success will motivate a person for repeated experimentation until, eventually, he will acquire the skill without realizing how this came about. This we usually attribute to nature, although it is largely the result of practice (*The Conduct of Human Understanding*). This description of the genesis of talent parallels his notion of how ideas come about. And this "attributing to nature" is the *idea innata* of Descartes; but Locke denies the existence of these. For him the mind is a *tabula rasa* at birth; only sensations beget ideas. Ideas of higher order, abstract ideas, arise through reflection, which connects the simple ideas.

Complex ideas, the products of reflection, shed light on the essence of reflection—which operates in the exact manner of associations, in that it connects ideas supplied by sensations. Our next task is to get acquainted with them.

III

. . . all our complex ideas, except those of substances, being archetypes of the mind's own making, not intended to be copies of anything, not referred to the existence of anything, as to their originals, cannot want any conformity necessary to real knowledge. . . . ideas of substances, which consisting of a collection of simple ideas, supposedly taken from the works of nature, may yet vary from them, by having more or different ideas united in them, than are to be found united in the things themselves: from whence it comes to pass that they may and often do fail of being exactly conformable to things themselves [(10) IV, 4, 5].

Our complex ideas of *substances* . . . are no further real than as they are such combinations of simple ideas as are really united, and so co-exist in things without us [(9) II, 30, 4].

Thus, complex ideas are very doubtful as regards correspondence to reality. Locke himself notes:

. . . the having the idea of any thing in our mind, no more proves the existence of that thing, than the picture of a man evidences his being in the world, or the visions of a dream make thereby a true history [(10) IV, 11, 1].

Reflection, then, whose essence is connecting and analyzing (analyzing makes ideas clear, connecting produces complex ideas), connects ideas in such a way that we have no guarantee that we will know reality by them. The problem of reflection, then, raises the same question as that of association. This fact will appear even more prominently if we examine the conditions for the confusion of complex ideas.

Some ideas are so complex . . . that memory does not easily retain the very same precise combination of simple ideas under one name [(9) II, 29, 12].

The defaults which usually occasion this confusion . . . are . . . first when any complex idea is made up of too small a number of simple ideas, and such only as are common to other things whereby the differences that make it deserve a different name are left out . . . secondly . . . when, though the particulars that make up any idea are in number enough, yet they are so jumbled together that it is not easily discernible whether it more belongs to the name that is given it than to any other . . . thirdly . . . when any one [idea] is uncertain and undetermined [(9) II, 29, 7].

Confusion making it a difficulty to separate two things that should be separated, concerns always two ideas [(9) II, 29, 11].

These conditions of confusion are purely the conditions of associative connections.

The answer lies in the real and nominal essence of substances. Locke knew of two kinds of essence. The real essence is the unknowable but real nature of things. The scholastic concept of "form" and the Kantian *"Ding an sich"* meet in this concept. The nominal essence, on the other hand, is made up of the characteristics and relationships that are known to us about a thing, of their effect on other objects, and of the effect other objects have on it. These are partly incidental, partly only gradually empirically knowable. In our own terminology, the nominal essence comprises everything that can be connected or associated with an object. Thus, according to Locke, there is no rigid substantial form to which complex ideas conform—we are given only the nominal essence. Therefore, objects, although not knowable in their real essence, may be classified and thus be at our disposal. Consequently things are known to us merely in their ascending order; that is, in their finality. Locke described the arrangement according to nominal essence as follows:

> Nature makes many *particular things*, which do agree one with another in many sensible qualities, and probably too in their internal frame and constitution; but it is not this real essence that distinguishes them into species; it is men who, taking occasion from the qualities they find united in them, and wherein they observe often several individuals to agree, range them into sorts, in order to their naming, for the convenience of comprehensive signs; under which individuals, according to their conformity to this or that abstract idea, come to be ranked as under ensigns; so that this is of the blue, that the red regiment; this is a man, that a drill; and in this, I think, consists the whole business of genus and species ([10] III, 6, 36).

I do not deny but nature, in the constant production of particular beings, makes them not always new and various, but very much alike and of kin one to another; but I think it nevertheless true that the boundaries of the species, whereby men sort them, are made by men; since the essences of the species, distinguished by different names, are, as has been proved, of man's making, and seldom adequate to the internal nature of the things they are taken from [(10) III, 6, 37].

It is clear that reflection is a psychic activity similar to association. However, reflection, which creates the idea of substances, is simply an association by similarities. Nominal essence arranges things according to concepts on the basis of collectively found similar qualities, irrespective of their real essences. This was recognized by Windelband:

How could the assimilation of sensory experiences in the human mind have a claim upon their real knowledge if our concepts are first stored in the memory, then related to one another by the associative connections of comparison, discrimination, joining and separation, so that finally the abstracting activity of thinking may form concepts of them and they may precipitate in language [(5), pp. 263–264].

Windelband's question is exactly our next problem. Associations have proved to be the generators of complex ideas. The concepts of reflection and association coincide. But this concept of association is not a mechanism, as it was for Hobbes; it is not just a source of confusion to be avoided, as it was for Descartes and Bacon. Although its reality value is problematical, it is the author of the act of understanding. For Locke there were no "forms" or *ideae innatae* to serve as firm foundations of the understanding. The associational mechanism of connecting and separating extended to the entire field of psychic phenomena. We have therefore to ask how Locke could regard this reflection of doubtful reality as the foundation of understanding. Which connecting created by reflection did he hold to be "natural"? In what way does the examination of the origin of an idea—the genetic analysis of psychic content—lead to the understanding of the reality of ideas?

IV

The answer to these questions can be found in one passage in the *Essay*: "We as plainly find the difference there is between any idea revived in our minds by our memory and actually coming into our minds by our senses, as we do between any two distinct ideas" ([10] IV, 2, 14).

However difficult it would be to defend this thesis against our present understanding of the problem, it still supplies the fixed point that allowed Locke to entrust himself to complex ideas acquired through reflection and to nominal essence as a source of true knowledge. After this statement of Locke's the question still remains what made this clear distinction possible? Locke's answer is: practice and intuition. Practice and intuition constitute the two poles of Locke's system. Practice is the highest criterion of empiricism. Empiricism (more exactly sensualistic empiricism) is the point of departure of Locke's system. Intuition is its climax of understanding: with it Locke far surpasses empiricism in the ordinary sense.

If anyone says "A dream may do the same thing and all these ideas may be produced in us without any external objects," he may please to dream that I make him this answer: (1) That it is no great matter whether I remove his scruple or no; where all is but dream, reasoning and arguments are of no use, truth and knowledge nothing. (2) That I believe he will allow a very manifest difference between dreaming of being in the fire, and being actually in it. . . . we certainly find that pleasure or pain follows upon the application of certain objects to us, whose existence we perceive, or dream that we perceive, by our senses; this certainly is as great as our happiness or misery, beyond which we have no concernment to know or to be [(10) IV, 2, 14].

According to this anti-Cartesian standpoint, then, practice indicates the difference between the various psychic contents. There are several possible ways of utilizing sensations: fantasy, dream, understanding. Each of these is built up of experiential data from sensations. But only understanding enables us to discover reality, because understanding alone can refer us directly to the real order. Each of these is produced by reflection. According to Locke, genetic examination can always demonstrate what kind of sensory data are present. Genetic examination shows the sensory data, while practice verifies knowledge. But, aside from practice, is there no other method or act that can distinguish between knowledge and other psychic content?

V

According to Locke, there is such an act; he calls it intuition.

There are three degrees of knowledge: sensation, demonstration, and intuition ([10] IV, 2, 1–13). This is Spinoza's heritage. Sensation, the simple ideas and their epistemological value are already known to us. Locke explains intuition as follows:

> For if we will reflect on our own ways of thinking, we will find that sometimes the mind perceives the agreement or disagreement of two ideas *immediately by themselves,* without the intervention of any other; and this, I think, we may call *intuitive knowledge.* For in this the mind is at no pains of proving or examining, but perceives the truth, as the eye doth light, only by being directed towards it. . . . when the mind cannot so bring its ideas together as, by their immediate comparison and, as it were, juxtaposition or application one to another, to perceive their agreement or disagreement, it is fain, by the *intervention of other ideas* (one or more, as it happens) to discover the agreement or disagreement which it searches, and this is that which we call *reasoning.* Now, in every step reason makes in demonstrative knowledge, there is an intuitive knowledge of that agreement or disagreement . . ." [(10), IV, 2, 1–7].

Intuition, accordingly, is the basic act of the mind that establishes similarities and differences. We have to ask how this specific function differs from what Fracastoro

called subnotio, because it is self-evident that the formation of concepts examined in connection with the nominal
essence could have happened only intuitively. Therefore,
what Locke called intuition, later associational philosophy
called association by similarity. The mental forces which
can distinguish between similar and dissimilar objects by
forming groups according to degrees of likeness cannot
in this system (in which the formation of such groups is
identical with the formation of concepts) be anything
but a basic and general, though not completely clarified,
version of associations by similarity. This will be even
clearer when we consider the operation of "demonstration." Locke himself says little about the essence of
intuition—he only went into detail on its general effect.
But it is an established fact for us that it is a form of
reflection, which—because of its general nature—is essentially the foundation of all reflection. This is the only
thesis in Locke's system with a certain mechanistic tinge.
Its general nature and its mechanistic-automatic tendency made it possible for Locke to regard knowledge as
a function of reflection modifying sensation. Intuition
can discriminate between ideas; thus there is no reason
to fear that the variety of psychic content will make
knowledge impossible.

What is most remarkable in Locke's system is that he
sees in the associative connection partly the fundamental
mode of functioning of the mind, and partly the most
threatening—literally, maddening—danger to the mind's
discovering of the truth. Ultimately, this brought the
whole psychic field under a unified law, although Locke
was unaware that *associatio idearum* and reflection obey
the same law. Yet the construction of a unified lawfulness

agrees with Locke's empirical starting point and genetic method of analysis. This unique psychic law was not worked out in its details. It was like any new step—faltering and full of misconceptions; yet it was the impetus for a new development.

VI

We have seen in the foregoing that Locke's concept of understanding was deeply rooted in empiricism. The following outline of the concept of understanding indicates how far and in what sense Locke transcended the traditional limitations of empiricism by aid of the intuition. For, if we examine the analysis given above, it will appear that intuition is but empiricism extended to cover the psychic realm. Consistently applied, empiricism transcends itself and for just this reason creates hypotheses and becomes science, true knowledge. The essence of this knowledge, according to Locke, is as follows:

. . . general certainty is never to be found but in our ideas. Whenever we go to seek it elsewhere, in experiment or observation without us, our knowledge goes not beyond particulars. It is the contemplation of our own abstract ideas that alone is able to afford us general knowledge [(10) IV, 6, 16].

Since the mind has no other immediate object but its own ideas . . . it is evident that our knowledge is only conversant about them. Knowledge seems then to me to be nothing but *the perception of the connection of and agreement, or disagreement and repugnancy of any of our ideas* [(10) IV, 1, 1].

. . . this agreement or disagreement . . . we may reduce . . . to . . .

    I. *Identity,* or *diversity.*

    II. *Relation.*

    III. *Co-existence,* or *necessary connection.*

    IV. *Real existence* [(10) IV, 1, 3].

. . . keep to the same precise ideas . . . without being led away by their names . . . separate the idea under consideration from the sign that stands for it . . . in the discovery of real truth . . . [(10) IV, 4, 9].

Thus, truth is correct connection and separation of signs.

After this he asks the following question: If our knowledge of things is sense-derived and if general knowledge consists in the dovetailing of ideas, what is the role of reason? His answer: the task of reason is to increase knowledge and to direct our assent. Thus the four steps in demonstration are the work of reason. They are: (1) discovering truths, (2) putting them in proper order and discovering their relationships, (3) noting correspondences, (4) drawing correct conclusions.

It seems as if reason were a new factor in the Lockean system. But careful examination shows that this new factor is compounded of two already known activities of psychic life: reflection and intuition. Although in its appearance it is autonomous, its constitution is associative. This is evident in Locke's example, [(10), pp. 393–394], in which he illustrates the steps of demonstration as follows:

Let this be the proposition laid down, "Men shall be punished in another world," and from thence be in-

ferred this other, "Then men can determine themselves," [(10) IV, 17, 4].

. . . what it is shows the force of the inference . . . but
a view of the connection of all the intermediate ideas
that draw in the conclusion . . .? E.g. "Men shall be
punished"; "God the punisher"; "Just punishment";
"The punished guilty"; "Could have done otherwise";
"Freedom"; "Self-determination"; . . . [(10) IV, 17, 4].

But these are in fact associated thoughts belonging to
the two poles. Thus demonstration begins with the discovery of the associated thoughts. Intuition decides which
are identical; by its aid they are arranged in a sequence,
every member of which is identical with its neighbor. The
result is that all intermediate ideas, being identical with
the thesis, interpret a certain part of it. The intermediate
ideas clarify the respective positions of parts of the main
idea (thesis) by associations and lead to the conclusion
by the series of identities. Every step in the process of
demonstration has the force of intuitive certainty, whence
the sequence of identities yields the conclusion. We are
thus confronted here by a broadened operation, compounded of associative elements. This is supported by
the fact that, according to Locke, demonstration is false
if the arrangement is accomplished by the wrong principles. These incorrect principles are wrong connections
made in childhood and on which we insist and the
passions which dominate us—as for instance, for a miser
the gold coin on the scale will outweigh anything else:
"*quod volumus, facile credimus.*" And these belong to the
category of *associatio idearum.*

VII

Locke, then, subsumes the entire realm of mental life under a single law. He himself was unaware of this in the *Essay*. His genetic, empirical approach, with the force of its inner logic, led him to this.

Given his empirical starting point, Locke's inner experience of recognizing associations prompted him to discover intuition. He is just as little dogmatic about associations as he is about external empiricism. The concept of reflection is free of any mechanism. His concept of intuition is an elastic experiment for the scientific formulation of psychic reality. Essentially we have to regard this system as the first attempt to describe psychic life in genetic terms. His genetic approach consists essentially of description, and his description is based on the presupposition of genetic analysis. The background of it all is the dynamism of desires and affections. The perception of these driving forces of psychic phenomena is so strikingly profound that in our age only Lewin's affective psychology can penetrate to similar depths.

Locke's work procured the raw material from which at a later date the complex stratification of the association concept emerged, well suited to render all mechanistic conceptions of association illusory. For this reason, Locke is in every sense of the word, closest to the picture we now have of associations.

Leibniz: The Metaphysical Phylogenesis of Being and the Unconscious

I

WINDELBAND AND CASSIRER regarded Leibniz's psychology as a construction deductively arrived at from his metaphysics. Révész (22) also started out from that perspective in analyzing Leibniz's psychology. The deductive character of Leibniz's system and the fact that it was bequeathed to us only in the form of mosaic-like treatises, indeed seems to favor such a view. But if we examine the role of associations in Leibniz's system, certain doubts arise as to the correctness of that interpretation.

To decide the question we must take a short glance at the problem of the relationship between being and consciousness. For the theories of association have been constant companions to this problem.

Here an opportunity offers itself to establish the philosophical-epistemological place of our investigations. We must not create the impression that the clarification of the problem of associations is in itself suitable to solve the momentous problem of the relationship between being and consciousness. But it is a fact that the thread of the history of the concept of association has always appeared simultaneously with the consciousness-being problem and that this simultaneity has not been properly appreciated in epistemological investigations. Yet associations are an inevitable stratum of psychic life, and every introspective speculation has to penetrate them either by taking an active stand on them or by submitting to their effect.

It is particularly characteristic of eras of enlightenment that the question of consciousness and being, and with it the problem of associations, is brought to the fore. The epoch of enlightenment of Greek skepticism and the respective stages of the less-well-known oriental philosophies all bear witness to this relationship.

II

The question of being and consciousness consists in this: how far can our consciousness reflect, or know, external being. Posing the question this way also explains the central role of associations. Insofar as a philosophical system ascribes autonomous activity to the thinking spirit, or mind, associations will have a place in this autonomous activity. Thus the question arises how an activity of the self could reflect external reality. In other words, how can one reach the truth in spite of associations.

In a philosophical system, if the mind is not ascribed autonomous activity—that is, if the system regards associations as mere mechanism—then in this system the mind is just the associatively united complex of concepts. Thus associations will assume a central psychic significance—even a decisive epistemological influence. All other possible solutions range between these two extremes.

Bacon hoped to show that in consciousness an image corresponding to reality arises from an increasingly wider understanding of reality, from the imprinting of reality into consciousness, and from a consistent (inductive) arrangement of such imprints.

Descartes found the solution in innate ideas, that is, in a priori concepts containing a blueprint of the principles of reality. Clearly and distinctly discerned, these retain their epistemological value in the mechanistic-associative operation of the mind.

Hobbes represents one extreme. For him sensual perception supplies the mechanism for reaching reality and the mind supplies the mechanism of forming concepts. And since, irrespective of the interrelationships of reality, *verum non in re sed in sensu constitit*, the associative mechanism of concepts replaces these interrelations of reality.

According to *Spinoza* every idea has a referent in the real world. If we want to avoid mistakes, we have to search out the correspondence in the proper order. Thus associations become the laws of both worlds—extended and conscious—in this system.

Locke attributed autonomous activity (reflection) to the human mind, and in order to clarify its influence he examines the psychogenesis of ideas. The result of his studies is that, unfortunately, to many of our ideas nothing at all corresponds in the external world—that they are simply associatively produced creations of the order-making efforts of the mind. He was the first to point out that the primary task of epistemology is to define the exact limitations of knowledge: to separate ideas that do correspond to reality from those that do not. After Locke, investigation continues in two directions: Leibniz represents one, Berkeley and Hume the other.

Berkeley tried to find an answer to the apparently insolvable problem of being and consciousness by making being immanent in consciousness. The images transmitted by the various senses are, according to him, held together by associative connections. General concepts are signs given by divine providence which warn men of events through the force of habit; that is, through associations.

Hume unified and completed Locke's and Berkeley's heritage. He accomplished the analysis of ideas as projected by Locke and found that all the basic concepts of knowledge are appearances produced by associative linkings. In the spirit of Berkeley's thought, Hume made the forms of knowledge the content of psychic operation; thereby associations reached the climax of their epistemological influence.

Leibniz, Locke's contemporary and critic, was—as we shall see—also the inheritor of some of his views. Yet he was at the same time a disciple of Descartes, Spinoza, and the modern occasionalists. The atmosphere in which he grew up was Descartes', emphasizing the duality of body and soul. He was not satisfied by Spinoza's or the occasionalists' solution. He searched for a deeper, unequivocal, and coherent solution of the problem of body and soul, of being and consciousness. The fruit of this search was the monad theory, which realized for the first time in modern philosophy the unity of being and consciousness, of body and soul. Looked at from this angle, the foundation of Leibniz's psychology definitely appears to be metaphysical. But our task is to examine the genesis of just this unbroken metaphysical conception and so get at its roots in personal experience and mental constitution.

III

Accordingly, our question is: Did his metaphysical monad theory or his theory of the unconscious appear first? Which constitutes the real core of Leibniz's system? Clearly, this question will be answered, not by chronological priorities but by the logical or, if one may put it that way, the psychological implications of these theories.

The theory of the unconscious and of the monads were fundamental in Leibniz's doctrine, as was noted by Hartmann (*Philosophie des Unbewussten*) and Révész (22). They are connected by the *harmonia praestabilita* and by the general principles of continuity and harmony. Of these basic factors, the theory of monads is undoubtedly not derived from experience. The discovery of the unconscious is—as we will see—still experienced by thinking men everywhere and this must have been so for Leibniz himself. The principles of continuity and *harmonia praestabilita* contain elements from both experience and speculation. It is easy to understand upon what basis Leibniz could pronounce the principle that nothing can be imparted to the mind that was not preexistent therein. He wrote: "The Monads have no windows, through which anything could come in or go out . . . Thus neither substance nor accident can come into a Monad from outside" ([11] 7).

After all, was not Leibniz the most outstanding polyhistor of his age! Each phenomenon in the real world and each theory he encountered, elicited from him an almost preformed view; everything that came up before his mind was an old acquaintance. The familiarity of relationships and things—this peculiar anamnesis is experienced by homo sapiens to this day. This experience necessarily drove Leibniz toward the hypothesis of an inner psychic phenomenon which works unconsciously in us:

> . . . each perception of the soul includes an infinite number of confused perceptions, which involve the whole universe. Each soul knows the infinite, knows all, but confusedly . . . Our confused perceptions are the result of the impressions which the whole universe makes on us [(13) 13].

Speculation had hardly begun to assimilate the original experience, and therefore at this point Leibniz faced the problem of *déjà vu*, of unconscious experience, which has been subjected to concrete investigation by Pötzl and others in our day. But Leibniz could not proceed in the same direction. For him, the problem of knowledge and experience was set against the background of Descartes' and Spinoza's philosophy and occasionalism. He could use the discovery of the unconscious itself only between these poles. And in fact he employed this discovery to resolve the difficulties presented by these systems. Because, if man possesses certain unconscious perceptions of reality, the extended and thinking substance no longer has its Cartesian duality in the sense of Spinoza's parallelism or in the sense of the perpetuating miracle of the occasionalists: body and soul make up a unit. He thus left unexploited the empirical-geometrical opportunity opened up by the discovery of the unconscious. He employed the genetic method designed by Locke in a way completely different from Locke's original intention. Locke's analysis is coupled with Leibniz's infinitesimal calculus. The result of the final analysis of ideas and of the indivisible, unified, basic substance of soul and body is the monad. This train of thought still contained one experiential datum: continuity. Its examination lies outside of the domain of our present investigations.

The problem of the unconscious and of the monads leads us to associations. But this monad is the child of Spinozism and occasionalism. That is why there is no interrelation among monads—only preestablished harmony.

We may see then that speculative considerations, determined by the prevailing philosophical climate of the age, were added to these two basic experiential facts; these characterize the ultimate form of Leibniz's doctrine and with it the attributes of the monads. In his terminology, Leibniz did not strictly conform to the principle of preestablished harmony. He often spoke of experience, effects, etc., whereas on the basis of preestablished harmony he could only operate with parallel preestablished masses of change. Leibniz himself perceived this inconsistency and excused it by saying that the Copernicans also spoke of the sun setting, while—as regards their system—that was an inconsistency. In spite of that explanation, we can assert that the terminological inconsistency bespeaks the speculative origin of monads and of preestablished harmony. This fact sheds light on how in philosophy experiential and personal factors are merely turning points of philosophical systems—the material content and form of these systems being determined by the intellectual perspective of the epoch and an over-determining multitude of historical influences. That is the fate of the problem of association in Leibniz's philosophy.

IV

For Leibniz, the changes in the monads were pre-established; thus associations could not constitute the autonomous activity of the soul, of which it might be asked how it could perform the task of understanding. The fundamental question of the methodology of understanding consists of the problem of clear versus obscure, and of confused versus definite, concepts. Leibniz supplemented these with the pairs corresponding–noncorresponding and symbolic–intuitive. (*Meditationes de cognitione, veritate et ideis.*) We have demonstrated in the examination of Descartes' theory of association that clear and distinct ideas are free from the disturbing effects of associations, while obscure and confused concepts are rendered such by that disturbing influence. Leibniz adopted the significance attributed to these concepts by Descartes without effecting any changes and connected them to the unconscious.

A monad has perceptions, but these perceptions are mostly confused ([11] 49). ". . . a feeling is something more than a bare perception . . . the name *souls* should be given only to those in which perception is more distinct and is accompanied by memory" ([11] 19). The mutual relationships of this obscurity and distinctness and those of associations are clarified by Leibniz's view on animal cognition:

. . . memory provides the souls with a sort of *consecutiveness* which resembles reason but which is to be distinguished from it. Thus we see that when animals have a perception of something which strikes them and of which they have formerly had a similar perception, they are led by means of representation in their memory to expect what was combined with the thing in this previous perception and they come to have feelings similar to those they had on the former occasion. For instance when a stick is shown to dogs they remember the pain it had caused them and howl and run away [(11) 26].

In the *New Essays*, he formulated this view even more sharply: ". . . brutes have perception, and . . . it is not necessary that they have thought, that is to say . . . have reflection or what may be its object" ([12] II, 9, 1). Then, in the same passage, he extended his investigations to man: "Also we ourselves have minute perceptions of which we are not conscious. It is true that we could very well perceive them, and reflect on them, if we were not turned aside by their multitude, which distracts our minds, or if they were not effaced or rather obscured by the greater ones" (*ibid.*).

While these passages only outline the relationships in question—showing that the significance of obscure concepts was the same for Leibniz as for Descartes—in the following Leibniz characterized obscure perceptions of animals in the same way as human associations: "The brutes pass from one imagination to another by the connexion which they have felt here before. . . . And on many occasions children, as likewise other men, have no other

procedure in their passages from thought to thought"
([12] II, 11, 11). And then he put it even more sharply:

> Each monad, with a particular body, makes a living
> substance. There is . . . an infinity of degrees in the
> monads, some dominating more or less over others . . .
> There is clearness and distinctness . . . in the im-
> pressions and consequently in the perceptions which
> represent these . . . this may lead to *feeling*, that is, to
> a perception accompanied by *memory* . . . And
> such . . . is called an *animal* and its monad is called a
> *soul* . . . It is true that animals are sometimes in the
> condition of simple living beings, and their souls in
> the condition of simple monads, namely when their
> perceptions are not sufficiently distinct to be remem-
> bered, as happens in a deep dreamless sleep, or in a
> swoon . . . Thus it is well to make distinction between
> *perception* . . . and *apperception* [(13) 4].

> There is a connexion among the perceptions of ani-
> mals which bears some resemblance to reason: but it
> is founded only in the memory of *facts*, or effects and
> not in the knowledge of *causes* . . . And men, insofar
> as they are empirics, that is to say, in the three-fourth
> of their actions act simply as the brutes do [(13) 5].

His conception about associations is summarily clarified in the following two quotations:

> It is not in the object, but only in the modification of
> the knowledge of the object that monads are limited.
> They all tend confusedly toward the infinite, toward

the whole; but they are limited and differentiated by the degrees of their distinct perceptions [(11) 60].

Our knowledge is of two kinds, distinct or confused. Distinct knowledge, or *intelligence*, occurs in the actual use of reason; but the senses supply us with confused thoughts. And we may say that we are immune from bondage in so far as we act with a distinct knowledge, but that we are the slaves of passion in so far as our perceptions are confused [(14') 289].

These passages need no analysis. They show the influence of Spinoza and are covered by the interpretation we gave of Spinoza's system. In the system of Leibniz they expressed the relation of the stage of the development of the monads to associations.

To sum up, we can say that according to Leibniz the history of the origin of being is the history of the establishment of the monads—of how the monad-organisms come about and how perceptions are transformed into apperceptions, the unconscious into the conscious. This relationship was pointed out by Windelband ([5] p. 292). And it is no other than the transformation of the indefinite into the definite, of the obscure into the clear; that is, the conversion from associative, habitual relationships into necessary truths. By this Leibniz lifted Descartes' conception of association, the disturbing effect of the body via associations, out of the pathological, attributing to it a general evolutionary significance by introducing the concept of "petites perceptions," or the unconscious. With this he also realized Locke's program, the genetic examination of ideas. Leibniz's train of thought anticipates, in a metaphysical form, the modern phylogenetic theories.

Leibniz's "new system" may be characterized as follows. It is based on the experience of the unconscious and of the associations, from which concepts emerge without the intervention of consciousness and thinking. The speculative explanation of these is uniform: all being is built up of the same basic elements—the monads—whose chief characteristic is perception. The perception of each monad represents all the other monads, and the change of these perceptions follows the changes of the other monads in the preestablished fashion. The dissimilarity of various monads consists in the different degrees of clearness in perceptions. The larger group of monads is subordinate to central monads, such as the soul. The clearer perceptions correspond to these greater complexities. The highest degree of these clearer perceptions is consciousness. Associative, habitual links are on a level preceding this. Man and animal consequently do not belong to two sharply separated categories. The disturbances of consciousness, Locke's *associatio idearum* bordering on psychosis, daydreaming, and sleep mean, to use a modern expression, regressions to previous, more obscure and chaotic, stages of perception. In this system, preexisting harmony and the monad theory are metaphysical speculations built on the phenomena of the subconscious and of associations. In these metaphysical forms a first, rather confused systematization of deep experiential intimations is developed.

In Leibniz's system psychic experience corresponds in a preestablished way with what happens to all the other monads. Thus psychological law would be given no place

alongside the physical laws—just as in Spinoza's system.
For Spinoza the source of error was the incomplete understanding of connections, so that the psyche was characterized at most by a narrow perspective pierced only by
intuition; but for Leibniz the clearness, distinctness, adequacy, and intuitiveness of perceptions vary according to
the various degrees of organization and differentiation.
Thus intuition becomes part of the genetic process: spir-
ituality, although constituted by the world of monads,
still involves evolution and regularity of a sort all its own.
Associative activity is an advanced, but not the most advanced, stage of perception. The lowest stages are the
various degrees of the *petites perceptions*; the highest the
rational understanding of validity—the ideas. All these
meant the recognition of a characteristic, phylogeneti-
cally interpreted unified psychic law which embraces the
totality of associations, the unconscious, absolute validity,
and the different degrees of clear, distinct, adequate, and
intuitive concepts. Leibniz thus created a unified psychic
law, the first in history, without leaving part of the
psychic life out of consideration. In the following we will
see that affective and impulsive life were not shut out
of his system either.

What is the motive force of associations according to
Leibniz?

For Bacon and Hobbes, the law of adhesion of association itself was the motor of psychic life. This view has
become paramount in the latest investigations concerning association. Physiological psychology started with the
assumption that all phenomena of psychic life can be
reduced to this mechanism designed after natural scientific models. But Descartes regarded other driving forces
as the origin of these associations. And for Locke and

Spinoza the creation of associations is bound up intimately with impulses and the affective life. This suggests that the concept of association evolved by the psychological mechanistic approach does not embrace the entire range of the problem. This remark establishes the basis of historical continuity with the latest phases in the study of associations. Spinoza's and Locke's conceptions are evident in Leibniz's works:

> We have an infinity of knowledge, of which we are not always conscious, not even when we have need of it. It is for memory to retain it and for reminiscence to represent it to us . . . And it must be that in this multiplicity of knowledge we are determined by something to renew some portion rather than another, since it is impossible to think distinctly and at once *of all that we know* [(12) 1, 5].

The action of the internal principle which causes the change or the passage from one perception to another, may be called *appetition*; it is true that the desire cannot always completely attain the whole perception which it strives for, but it always attains something of it, and reaches new perceptions [(11) 15].

The concept of appetition is defined in the *New Essays* as follows: "The uneasiness which a man feels in himself at the absence of anything which if present would give him pleasure is called desire" ([12] 1, 20, 6). And in the preface to the *New Essays* he traces back the origin of this uneasiness to the presence of perceptions. In the tense, restless, unpleasant state of uneasiness the influence of unrecognizable, unconscious perceptions is manifest.

Thus an impulse-dynamic factor is at the root of associations. But in Leibniz's system—and in any other rationalistic system, including those of Descartes and Spinoza—every instinctual impulsive activity is based on concepts, perceptions. This follows from the inner logic of the rationalistic system. Leibniz's doctrine contains the traces of impulsive-dynamic driving forces controlling associations, but in his system it is a topsy-turvy, rationalistic-impulsive dynamism.

VI

Our task now consists in clarifying the meaning Leibniz assigned to the term knowledge, in order to shed light on the influence of associations on the understanding.

Leibniz stood on the borderline between empiricism and rationalism. For him there was no empiricism without rational foundation. Cassirer demonstrated this and expressed his results as follows: "The concepts of size, shape, and motion render reality intelligible" ([1] p. 78).

For Leibniz the development of reason was impossible without empiricism: "In a sense, it may be said that the outward senses are the causes of our concepts" ([12] 1, 11). This interweaving of empirium and ratio broke through the speculation of preestablished harmony, the entire system of monads. These made up the metaphysical background which proved the validity of empirium and ratio. But in the foreground, independently of this even in terminology, the process of understanding progressed with the aid of the specific relationship between empirium and ratio.

The relation of the connection of empirium and ratio to associations can be seen from Leibniz's standpoint concerning innate ideas. It is unimportant, according to Leibniz, to decide whether a concept is innate or experientially acquired because, in the last analysis—in the final source of being—empiricism and reasoning are identical. Leibniz repeatedly refers to this question in the *New Essays*: "Thus ideas and truths are innate as inclinations, dispositions, propensities, natural powers, but not as finished activities" ([12] 25). Potential innatism replaces actual innatism, just as in modern instinctual psychology (for example, L. R. Müller), where empiricism and reason are bound inseparably. "We could know all the beauties of the world in every single soul if we were capable of opening each of its folds, which however open up perceptibly only in time."

Every confused and obscure perception contains the potential for pure knowledge of the world, only the time which would unfold it has not yet come. That is why the problem of innatism is meaningless. ". . . there must also be a sufficient reason for . . . truths of fact, that is to say, for the sequence or connexion of the things . . . in which the analyzing into particular reasons might go on . . ." ([11] 36).

Empiricism and associations make up one stage in the process of development they have to go through. Validity is inherent in them but it has not yet developed: only analysis can demonstrate the possibilities of their components—truth has not yet unfolded. The essence of ratio is contained in empirium. And this empirium is occasioned by associations: properties that are knowable through the senses are based on experience and possible only by comparison with previous experience.

The unity of experience and reason, then, flows from this: that in the phylogenesis of the perceptions, the highest perception—such as has absolute validity where the opposites of those necessary truths involve a contradiction ([11] 30–35)—is preceded by associations which contain the seeds of the highest stage.

Two problems of Leibniz's system shed particular light on this relationship between associations and reason; they show that Leibniz's "ratio" behaves as though it were but an associative function. First, Leibniz called for the establishment of a new logic which would take probabilities into consideration ([12] 4, 16, 9). This is a new datum in support of the fact, already known from the phylogenesis of perceptions, that necessary truths and associations are not two sharply separated domains. Second, Leibniz concluded that species which have no actual existence are logically still possible ([12] 3, 6, 12). This thesis states that the signs connected by the activity (ratio) of the mind do not necessarily define a phylum existing in the real world. But in this case reason falls into the same pit toward which associations always tended. Reason, thus, may at best prove the necessity of possibility but not the necessity of real being. This is in harmony with the view of Leibniz that sensation is the cause of our thoughts. In general, however, Leibniz maintained the necessary validity of reasoning. Windelband has shown that Leibniz's error consists exactly in his unfounded assumption that logical possibility is the foundation of being ([5] p. 473). As regards associations, this means that rational activity is capable of revealing the contradictions of associations, but it cannot demonstrate the *correspondence between associations and reality*; that can be achieved only by induction, the juxtaposition of experiential facts. This is our frequent everyday experience too.

By this latter train of thought, the concept of "adequate ideas," with which Leibniz complemented the Cartesian concepts of "clear and distinct ideas" with relation to associations, was given an interpretation. The other complementing pair—symbolic and intuitive concepts—was still to be interpreted.

VII

Intuitive knowledge refers to that which the mind understands through concentration and mere observation. But where this is not possible, because the mind is incapable of viewing the multiplicity of the object in a unified fashion, the object is given a name, a sign, a symbol; from then on intelligence works with that symbol. Cassirer demonstrated in his work *Philosophie der symbolischen Formen* that symbolism, symbolical knowledge, is the most ancient form of knowledge. It is the substitution of objects, concepts, and thoughts for those signals, words, and images that have been most closely associated with them—by similarity. The essence of symbolization is that we substitute the simple for the complex, on which we are not able to focus our attention as on a single unit; the one-dimensional for the multidimensional; the idea having a single undetermined aspect for the multiply undetermined; the sensory for the formless spiritual; the visually perceptible for the nonvisual haptic. In short, we project them on a plane. Leibniz knew this. He wrote: "Although the idea of a circle is not similar to a real circle, one can deduce truths from the former that can be proved from experience" ([13] p. 263). For him, the idea is not identical with or similar to the object; it is only its sign. In this case, mathematics served as a model. He used the same idea to solve the Molineaux problem. Leibniz was certain that a blind man who regained his vision would not recognize a sphere or cube he merely felt before. But he was also convinced that if the blind man knew he had the cube and the sphere before him he would be able to tell them apart ([12] 1, 9, 8). Consequently, the idea the man formulated when he could not see did not resemble the sphere or the cube. His concepts of these forms were neither clear nor distinct. He could not really know them, but he could infer them by associations, because he perceived some of their signs, which are sufficient under conditions of limited choice. These signs are the eight corners of the cube he could feel and the roundness of the sphere, which exclude each other. When he, on some level of perception, could *see* these together, he would know which one had to be associated with the already obtained perception. But were he to see either form alone, his idea obtained through his tactile sense would be inadequate for the task. This situation is analogous to the situation we have in case of symbolical knowledge.

We see then that there are associative connections at the core of symbolical knowledge. Undoubtedly, it was primarily this that Leibniz had in mind. One type of symbolical knowledge, the mathematical, has a high degree of validity. Mathematics works with symbols, yet its results acquaint us with real relationships. Leibniz did not achieve an explanation of the meaning of this correspondence. The quotation about the circle suggests the idea that we apply the inferences drawn from the concept "circle" to a real configuration, which verifies those inferences. Leibniz did not draw this conclusion, even though it would have been in harmony with his rationalism. Modern rationalists, the school of mathematical formal-ism, hold that mathematics is true in itself insofar as it does not deal with reality; but insofar as it does, it is not necessarily truc (Hilbert, von Neumann). This conviction is a direct consequence of the abovementioned inference. But the question has not been clarified and is a disputed point among contemporary intuitionists, logicians, and formalists.

Starting out from the marvellous results of mathematics, Leibniz hoped to establish a general science that would evolve new theses in all branches of science by the operations performed with symbols. He considered the following as the basic tenet of such a universal characteristic: a thing is to be regarded as the expression of another only if a constant and regulated relationship exists between the statements that can be made about them ([14] pp. 238, 241). I think it is apparent that by this he sought to replace the confused associative connections of symbolization with adequate, rational, regular, and necessary forms. Accordingly, he wanted to create a higher, more general level of perception, hitherto not attained by the human monad, which would approximate perfection and in which "all analysis would be performed and thus everything that for us is experiential and habitual would appear necessary"—for nothing is without a cause ([12] 5, 1, 21 and 13). This project remained unfinished. Its substantial nature is indicated by the fact that today topology and set theory—but above all Russell, Carnap, and their collaborators—tread the same path.

VIII

In this system, then, associations play an important role, even though this role is veiled by the metaphysical setting despite Leibniz's attempt to reconcile rationalism, empiricism, and even Spinoza's mysticism, which introduced speculative elements that rendered clarification of the role difficult.

We have found that associations entertained an intimate link with the phenomenon of the unconscious, and we have observed that Leibniz's metaphysics stemmed from the combined effect of these two factors. Associations appeared because of the Cartesian heritage, as perceptions corresponding to a lower degree of development. In this capacity they achieved the harmony of empiricism and rationalism.

The systematizing mind of Leibniz treated associations under the label of the continuity of consciousness. He made them an indivisible factor in the development of perceptions and, by creating this continuity, produced the first rounded psychological system extending over the entire psychic domain.

Berkeley: Solipsistic Idealism Without Abstract Ideas

I

WE MAY SHED LIGHT on the significance of Berkeley's system by a historical retrospection.

Bacon regarded associations as merely a disturbing effect that impedes the grasping of reality. Induction was meant to get rid of the teleology of generalization—the idols—through existing reality.

Descartes penetrated more deeply into the web of associations. Beyond particular idols—of which he was cognizant—the disturbing effect of associations forced him to doubt every form of thought. Consequently, he accepted as valid knowledge only the self—the apparently firm basis of all connections—and the *ideae innatae*—which remain unchanged amidst changing connections. By this he brought about the dualism of body as opposed to ratio. Ratio is a clear and trustworthy source of knowledge, while the body, through its passions and emotions, generates associative connections, which confuse and obscure things.

Hobbes was the first deliberately to make associations consciously the basic mechanism of psychic life. It is natural that by this act associations become the indispensable mechanical originators of knowledge. This automatic cognitive process depicts, according to Hobbes, the senses and not the external world: *verum non in re, sed in sensu constitit.* Thus is sensualism occasioned; in it the external world is the cause of sensations, but theoretical unity and connection exist only in the associatively produced laws of sensations. Cartesian dualism no longer obtains, though it is not eliminated.

In the system of Spinoza, Cartesian dualism attains its climax. Physical and spiritual spheres coexist without any connection or interaction whatsoever, but they are in harmony since both are attributes of the divine substance. For Spinoza associations represent a part of the general divine law, because in the world, which is identical with God (*Deus sive natura*), everything is uniform. Associations—though they otherwise bind with the force of law—may induce error, but only if we are unable to perceive their place in the whole, if we refer them to the wrong position. This law-making role of associations—in which every connection, whether actually thought of or thinkable, has something corresponding to it in the real world —conceived, in a way that is both daring and mystical, of being as a dual unity.

In Locke's system, Baconian empiricism and the effort to set itself free of idols (*associatio idearum*) meet with elements taken over from Hobbes' sensualism. The dualism of sensation and reflection thus created—which Locke regarded as the basis of his psychology—became the foundation for a new dualism. Spinoza's notion was that each idea, each associatively occasioned thought, has something corresponding to it in the world of objects; it only has to be found in the correct way. With Locke this is transformed into the search for the experiential origin of ideas. Because, according to him, that is the sole valid means of finding that connection in reality to which the association of ideas refers. For Locke again, then, the duality of the real world and the knowing mind subsists in full force in the form of sensation and reflection. A genetic analysis, the examination of reflection, leads from associatively acquired ideas to the original sensation. For Locke, these are two worlds; true knowledge is based on reconciling them. But this can come about only with simple ideas and through the mediation of intuition. In general, however, this system is characterized by a dogged effort to discover correspondences and a frequent avowal of the lack of them. This dualism is reconciled by Berkeley and Hume.

II

Let us see, then, how Berkeley attacked the problem. His early diary, *Commonplace Book*, shows that he too started out from sensualism. "We must with the mob place certainty in the senses" ([15"] 1, 44). "Foolish in men to despise the senses. If it were not for them, the mind could have no knowledge, no thought at all" ([15"] 1, 23). This view persisted through all phases of Berkeley's development. Accordingly, instead of the idealistic notion of the spontaneity of the mind, only the concept of thinking produced by sensation was known to Berkeley.

Essays Toward a New Theory of Vision delineates the path of his development. Here too the basis of knowledge consists of sense impressions, though these are of two kinds: ideas perceived through the senses and ideas suggested by other ideas. Strictly speaking, the latter are not ideas but fancies. Berkeley strove to separate the ideas gained purely through sensations. By this he founded the trend to examine "pure perceptions." According to Berkeley, all other concepts are "suggested" by these pure perceptions. In this sense, all general concepts, ideas, etc., are "suggested." As we shall see, Berkeley arrived at an idealistic system in his inferences. Yet the spiritual climate of "pure perceptions" bound him, and thus he created a system of idealism in which abstractions or ideas have no validity. Apart from the basic principle of the divinity, it is only "pure perception" that is not "suggested." Concepts, abstractions, relationships, the basic forms of knowing and reflection, are all "suggested." That is how idealism without ideas was produced.

The most characteristic product of these researches is the concept of "suggestion." About this, *Essays Toward a New Theory of Vision* notes, ". . . there are no abstract ideas of figure . . . and it is impossible for us, by any precision of thought, to frame an idea . . . separate from all other visible and tangible qualities . . ." ([15] 5, 127).

This method of linking is a classic form of association. The line of thought in the *Essays* unequivocally shows that suggestion essentially corresponds to the concept of association. For the core of the *Essays* is that vision does not determine distance or the absolute and relative sizes of objects by geometric operations performed in the visual organ and does not turn the images upside down by those operations. The various degrees and qualities of tactile sensations are linked to the various degrees of the impressions and motions of the eye by experience and habit— that is to say, associatively. As a result of these associative connections, the impressions of the visual organ suggest the concepts of distance, size, and straight line

([15] 17, 52–60). This shows that space is a suggested concept. But Berkeley went even farther and considered the concept of object to be suggested as well: "And as several of these [ideas] are observed to accompany each other, they come to be marked by one name, and so to be reputed as one *thing*" ([16] 1, 1).

The concepts of relation, then, are suggested by the associative linking of visual and tactile sensations or ideas; the concepts of objects, by the association of simultaneously arising sensations or concepts. Hume termed the latter association caused by coexistence.

The basis of knowledge is, accordingly, pure perception, and the forms of knowledge are produced by suggestion (association).

III

Berkeley's idealism rests on the concepts of "pure perception" and "suggestion." Visual ideas "suggest" the ideas produced by the tactile sense; that is to say, the former involve the latter by the habitual, associative connection entertained between them. It is by no means necessary that the two kinds of idea be coexistent, for the connection is merely experiential. Thus we see here two things. One is the idea supplied by the senses—far, near. It is not identical with anything in the outside world because an idea can only be identical with another idea. The other kind of idea is in the mind but is only suggested—for instance the idea of distance ([15] 16–25).

Thus is the inherited dualistic strain dissolved. An idea can be identical only with another idea; accordingly ideas cannot be identical with external objects. "That it [the extended thing] exists not in the mind is agreed; and that it exists not in place is no less certain—since all place or extension exists only in the mind . . . it remains therefore that it exists nowhere at all" ([16] 67). Material things as such, then, do not exist; even if they did, they could not be identical with ideas.

". . . the connection of ideas does not imply the relation of *cause and effect*, but only of a mark or *sign* with the *thing signified*. The fire which I see is not the cause of the pain I suffer upon approaching it, but the mark that forewarns me of it" ([16] 65). We have seen that the connection between ideas is associative and not based on absolute law. Berkeley developed this associative link into a teleological relation between sign and that which is signified to be made later into the instrument of providence in the hands of the immaterial principle of which the world has been fashioned.

The world exists only in the mind, and there, in the concepts of the mind, it is dual: it consists on the one hand of real concepts and, on the other, of suggested ones. "The ideas imprinted on the senses by the Author of nature are called *real things*, and those excited in the imagination . . . are more properly termed *ideas* or *images* of *things* . . ." ([16] 33). By this, the basic problem of idealism has been solved—the problem of how interior events become exterior. In this solution associations play a decisive part. External and internal are the same, for everything exists in the mind only. The immaterial, spiritual principle ruling over the spiritual construction thus produced uses the mechanism of associations as an instrument of its providence. It assists us by giving warning signals so that we be not at the mercy of the next moment.

The role of associations is dual in this system: they

create concepts and objects, and they create a system of signs to call man's attention to dangers that loom over him. Associations are consequently instruments of both knowledge and providence. From this we might suppose that associations could never lead to error.

IV

That supposition would be incorrect, for Berkeley repeatedly mentions the possibility and the causes of error:

> This is not the only instance wherein men impose upon themselves, by imaging they believe those propositions which they have often heard, though at bottom they have no meaning in them [(16) 54].

> That one idea may suggest another to the mind, it will suffice that they have been observed to go together, without any demonstration of the necessity of their coexistence . . . [(15) 25].

These insights are surprising in Berkeley's system, for the above delineated division of concepts or ideas and the nonexistence of the world of material things seem to render the concept of error superfluous. Yet, if we consider these possibilities of error irrespective of Berkeley's system, we will recognize old acquaintances in them. The first one emerged with Descartes; the second is familiar from Bacon's idols. Only the third one appears in a somewhat new shape, although it reminds one of Lockean problems.

We have to point out, however, that the emergence of the question of error is in intimate connection with some other problems of Berkeley. He asks in paragraph 61 of the *Principles* why the Creator needs such a complicated machinery for the universe, when with His will alone he could keep the external empty framework of the world in the same shape as He is now keeping it by a complex machine. At the moment Berkeley's answer does not concern us. But the very emergence of the question indicates that Berkeley's system of spiritual monism contains two possibilities. In one the world is relatively autonomous—and in it error also has a place. In the other, it is not:

> . . . suffice from present phenomena and effects, through a chain of natural causes and subordinate blind agents, to trace a Divine Intellect as the remote original cause, that first created the world, and then set it a-going. We cannot make even one single step in accounting for the phenomena, without admitting the immediate presence and immediate action of an incorporeal agent, who connects, moves, as seem good to him [(15′) 237].

As a result of the second possibility, the significance of associations is lost. They are not a mere source of error as they were for Bacon; they do not become law, as with Spinoza. They stand closest to Hobbes' mechanism. But here the mechanism of the soul is not autonomous, sense perceptions are transformed by the imagination, as in Locke's system reflection was transformed by sensation. Finally they also admit the possibility of error, as in the Cartesian doctrine.

Berkeley reached beyond the conclusions of Hobbes. While Hobbes' sensualism is skeptical of the comprehensibility of the real world, for Berkeley, skepticism disappears with the existence of material reality ([16] 96). Berkeley drives Locke's inferences to their final conclusion: he finds that every reflection is "suggested" and only "pure sense" is reality. Associations, like everything else, play a subordinate role as regulated by the Creator's hand. He neglects to examine their mechanism. He does not even analyze the forms of their appearance or effect; he treats them as a subordinate instrument.

But associations are a stubborn instrument. Berkeley wishes to deprive them of their independence and they reappear as a source of error—as we have seen. Berkeley was forced to take note of that. This obliges him, as it did earlier Descartes, to return to the supposition of pure, autonomous reason—which he previously denied by rejecting abstract ideas. First he admits only that the imagination possesses a certain amount of freedom to change the position and relation of concepts given it by God ([1] pp. 235–236), but later on he recognizes a law proper to the individual mind. That is, under the error-inducing influence of associations, he turns toward the first possibility—mentioned above—namely, the autonomy of being. He takes the final step in this direction by acknowledging the validity of Plato's theory of ideas. His standpoint here reminds us of Descartes, who took refuge from the chaos of associations in the innate ideas. Berkeley states:

That philosopher held that the mind of man was a *tabula rasa*, and that there were no innate ideas. Plato, on the contrary, held original ideas in the mind; that is, notions which never were or can be in the sense, such as being, beauty, goodness, likeness, parity. Some, perhaps, may think the truth to be this: that there are properly no *ideas*, or passive objects, in the mind but what were derived from sense; but that there are also besides these her own acts or operations; such are *notions*.

It is a maxim of the Platonic philosophy, that the soul of man was originally furnished with native inbred notions, and stands in need of sensible occasions, not absolutely for producing them, but only for awakening, rousing, or exciting into act what was already preexistent, dormant, and latent in the soul; as things are said to be laid up in the memory, though not actually perceived until they happen to be called forth and brought into view by other objects. This notion seemeth somewhat different from that of innate ideas, as understood by those moderns who have attempted to explode them. To understand and to be are, according to Parmenides, the same thing. And Plato in his seventh Letter makes no difference between . . . mind and knowledge. Whence it follows that mind, knowledge, and notions, either in habit or in act, always go together ([15'] 308, 309).

Here, abstract ideas emerge as independent entities. This is opposed to his own point of departure, where he denies the existence of abstract ideas. We shall be able to survey this inner conflict in his philosophical development when examining more closely his argument against abstract ideas.

V

We have already mentioned that Berkeley considers any abstract idea impossible. This is understandable if we remember his starting point. This leads him to oppose sharply Locke's definition by exclusion, according to which the concept of the triangle is one "neither equilateral, nor isosceles, nor a right triangle, etc." Against this Berkeley notes: ". . . when I demonstrate any proposition concerning triangles, it ought . . . to be understood . . . that the particular triangle I consider, whether of this or that sort it matters not, doth equally stand for and represent all rectilinear triangles whatsoever, and is in that sense universal" ([16] Introduction, 15). Cassirer, who devotes considerable attention to this question, points out that representation in Berkeley's system is really an associative function, its role being the substitution of ideas one for the other and the expression of one by another. ([1] I, pp. 220–221).

Cassirer accordingly asserts that for Berkeley the genesis of concepts occurs through associative connections. He states, as if with resignation, "It seems that empirical concepts admit of no other interpretations and explanation than that contained in associations of concepts. These are collections of notes connected only by experiential affinities and not necessity" ([1] I, 225). According to Cassirer, then, Berkeley's formation of concepts was similar to Locke's notion of the origin of ideas. Cassirer here sharply criticizes Berkeley's conception and shows—as we have done above—that Berkeley's turning to Plato is a result of it. The essence of his view is as follows:

> It is not the range of a concept and the command thereof that is important, but the principle of selection. Similarity has to be perceived and judged. And these are mental functions . . . Analysis, subordination, and

dominance, the separation of the specific and contingent in the individual concept, the extrication of general relationships and of the permanent connections in thinking—all these cannot be the achievement of associations. These changes in the impressions can never be explained by associations, because with them there can be only arrangement, side by side, on the same level. By associations the differentiation of the meanings of particular components can never be achieved, although the root of the concept stems from this. No formal meaning can come from the mere piling up of components [(1) I, pp. 220–224].

Undoubtedly, Cassirer is correct as regards the usual sense of the concept of association. But how is this truth related to Cassirer's admission that the empirical concept dealt with by Berkeley can be conceived of only as a product of associations? Without a doubt, if Hobbes' algebra of image and concept, his mechanistic conception of association, are the same as the idea of association here described, then in this concept surely there are no elements by which one could explain how individual concepts, united by like elements contained in them, should become a unified concept. The formal appearance of the empirical concept nevertheless infers associations.

Our researches have already shown that the concept of association transcends the usual boundaries assigned to it by classic definitions.

Where we have probed deeper into the problem, it has turned out that associations are not determining factors but only forms of mental phenomena, behind which is hidden a dynamism, with affective and impulsive forces, determining the direction of associations. In this context we may point out that, with the remolding of the concept of association, this will reappear as the structure of the mental process; then it may justly claim recognition also as the mode of the formation of ideas. At this stage, however, Cassirer's criticism that it is impossible to conceive of associations as the motive force in the formation of concepts, is legitimate. Lewin's modern theory of associations essays to evolve a concept of association answering just these stipulations.

VI

Berkeley's philosophy makes other contributions to the evolution of the problem of association. The source of these is Berkeley's theory about image formation and concept formation.

Concept formation. We have seen that, according to Berkeley, the ideas of the visual and tactile senses do not necessarily relate to one and the same object, although they have an associative connection. These ideas do not correspond to one another as concerns their qualities, but only as concerns the number of their component parts. For instance, to each side of the triangle as seen corresponds a side of it as felt. This is the first appearance of the mathematical set-property of the concept. Hume evolved and expanded Berkeley's idea into a concept-forming operation which, as we shall see, is analogous to multiplication in set theory. In these philosophers' doctrines, as well as in multiplication in set theory, the elements common to the respective sets are the result of the operation. This opened the path for a qualitative mathematics which is not necessarily foreign to the nature of the phenomenon of consciousness—unlike Hobbes' concept-algebra, which *was* foreign to it. Set theory treats of infinite sets, of families with an infinite number of members; as a science it is the foundation of mathematics, and its position is next to that of logic. As such it is built immediately over the foundations of the laws of the mechanism of human mental activity. Owing to all these circumstances, it is well suited to provide psychology with an adequate terminology and descriptive flexibility. And this is a necessary prerequisite to a synoptic perspective and scientific examination of the psychic process. Modern psychological research has so far taken advantage only of topology to create such a terminology (Lewin, *Topological Psychology*).

Image formation. Berkeley's problems concerning vision, distance, and size of objects constitute the core of contemporary researches concerning constancy.

Berkeley's solution, which attributes the origin of our judgement of distance and size partly to the mechanism of the eye—that is, to a peripheral effect—and partly to associative—that is, central—relationships, is essentially similar to the results of the Adhemar Gelb constancy test. Gelb concludes:

Our world of vision is not built up of the raw material of primary sensations and complexes of sensation determined by stimuli and unassimilated, with the co-operation of higher (psychic) accessory processes, but our sensorium, to begin with, develops under conditions that according to our motivation and inner stimuli, we find around us a world of objects formed and articulated in this or that manner, at times richly and at times poorly [(28) 12, 1].

Both Berkeley and Gelb, then, see the foundation of concept formation in the unity of peripheral and central activities. And this unity was brought about during the development of the sensorium. The role of associations here described suggests that we may expect certain contributions from examinations of constancy toward a more highly differentiated concept formation of association.

In Berkeley's thought, then, associations play a part in establishing idealism. For him the instruments of object-constancy and concept formation were given by associative connections. He broadened pure perception and suggestion into a law extending over the entire mind. For the first time this law included the whole of the mind and with that the whole world. Later, the Platonic ideas become independent of these laws, just as the innate ideas did in Descartes' doctrine.

Hume: The Birth of Skepticism and Positivism

I

IN THE COURSE of our study we have so far witnessed the formation of two branches in the evolution of the history of the concept of association. One of these starts with Bacon and searches for the sources of the errors of the human mind in factors that could be conceived of as associations. This line has an offshoot in Descartes and continues with Hobbes, who develops the relationships in question into mechanisms. This line leads to Locke. In his system this mechanism develops into the concept of the association of ideas; it is deepened to a point where it virtually loses its mechanical nature. Later on Hartley, Priestly, and E. Darwin carry these investigations further, and then Priestly approaches materialism.

In the other direction, where associations are not merely a source of error but the basis of knowledge, the origins of this thinking are less clear. Fracastoro and Campanella studied the basic problems of knowledge; the processes they designated as the basic operations of concept formation, thinking, and sensation proved to be associative connections. But these Renaissance philosophers were far from a mechanistic conception about these processes. Their thinking influenced both Descartes' object-constancy theory and Hobbes' mechanistic perspective. But the nature of their relationship to the two great turning points of the line of evolution, Spinoza and Berkeley, is not clear. Associations first came into the center of interest with the problem of knowledge of Spinoza. In his system, they do not present themselves as mechanisms but as the necessary interrelationships valid both in thinking and in reality, which—when viewed in their entirety—are found to be infallible. Naturally, this perspective, by letting everything dissolve and *merge*, did not result in knowledge because it could not *connect* any things. For Berkeley, associations were instruments of providence issuing signs, creators of abstract ideas and of concepts of relationship. Historically, Locke is wedged between the two. He draws the final conclusion from the Cartesian conception of associations. With him the epistemological influence of associations reaches its climax and results in an overall picture not in the least mechanistic. The two branches, then, meet in Locke. The synthesis of associations as a source of error and as mechanism and also as the basis of the cognitive processes was created by Hume. While Locke's theory and ideas are not sharply outlined, for they were born in the crossfire of the different perspectives, in Hume the two directions are consciously unified. This synthesis is not yet free of contradictions—partly because that is the fate of every synthesis, and partly because, as we shall see, oftentimes the scientific instruments with which the attainment and consistency of the synthesis could have been attained were missing. Yet Hume's synthesis anticipates many basic formulations of problems in modern psychology.

II

The basic tenet of Hume's philosophy is this: to every idea or concept there corresponds an original impression. *"That all our simple ideas in their first appearance, are derived from simple impressions, which are correspondent to them, and which they exactly represent"* ([17] I, 1, 1, p. 4).

The source of this thesis is in Locke, but it took us a lengthy analysis to show it. In contrast, Hume provides us with a clear account of the grounds for his supposition. While Locke attempted to furnish the genesis of a few concepts only by way of illustration, Hume made these analyses into a closed system. He held that the basic problem of epistemology was to be found in the origin of the concepts of space, time, matter, object constancy, personal identity, and causation; that is why Hume's system stands or falls with the discovery of "impressions" corresponding to these. In place of the sensation-reflection scheme, Hume devised the impression-idea formula. By this he freed the meaning of reflection from its Lockean, equivocal quality. The concretization of the concept of reflection; the thorough investigation of the basic concepts of knowledge, space, time, matter, object constancy, personal identity, and causation; and through these the unequivocal formulation of the problem of knowledge opened up the road toward Kant.

Without the basic concepts of knowledge, the mechanism of thinking is incomprehensible, because, "When we say that an object is connected with another, we mean only that they have acquired a connection in our thought . . ." ([18] 7, 2, p. 631). This arises from temporal and spatial contiguity and causal connection. With the revaluation of the concept of object, Hume transcends the subjective character of Locke's empiricism. According to Locke, nothing can interest us that lies without the sphere of our own interests; we saw that for that reason he posited a sensualistic criterion of reality. But Hume ascends to an empirical-genetic view of reality through the associative interpretation of object constancy. The difficulties of Hume's system center on the problem of personal identity, the problem of the self. Hume knew that without the clarification of that question the problem of knowledge would remain suspended in mid-air. He gave the self a mechanical interpretation but, as we shall see, this interpretation did not satisfy him and he was often obliged to transcend the boundaries of this mechanism.

Though Hume stated that every idea comes from an original impression, he did not offer a proof of logical validity to support this thesis. He referred to experience when arguing that the original impression that corresponds to space is the juxtaposition of objects; to time, the succession of events; to causation, the simultaneous appearance of phenomena. If, for the time being, we disregard the more complicated analysis of the other basic cognitive concepts, we may summarize those we have already dealt with as demonstrating that concepts are created by habit, that is to say, by association. This makes it certain that for Hume the search for the history and original impression of ideas meant the examination of the associative mechanism, because it is this associative mechanism that makes us see the external world the way we actually do. At this point we witness the recurrence of the influence of Berkeley's concept of suggestion, although now adapted to Hume's empiricism. Hume repeatedly suggests that associations may be the source of errors ([17] I, 3).

> Should it be demanded why men form general rules, and allow them to influence their judgment, even contrary to present observations and experience, I should reply, that in my opinion it proceeds from these very principles on which all judgments concerning causes and effects depend. Our judgments concerning cause and effect are derived from habit and experience; and when we have been accustomed to see one object united to another our imagination passes from the first to the second by a natural transition which precedes reflection and which cannot be prevented by it. [(17) I, 13, p. 147].

It is clear from this that he regarded associations not as a source of error but as a mechanism of thinking. Hume sought in associations the universal laws of thinking and not a source of error, laws comprising both correct and incorrect thinking. He did not, like Descartes, take refuge from association in innate ideas; he did not, like Locke, wish to get rid of them as phenomena bordering on madness only to let them in through the back door. They became the conscious foundation of his reasoning and the pillar of his philosophical system. Now we shall make this role of the associations the subject matter of our examination.

III

All notions of the mind derive from impressions. This is the basis of Hume's universal laws of the psychic process. Historically, this is the first system of laws consciously to embrace all mental phenomena. Locke's similar effort remained mere contemplation; only detailed analysis could show that that view pervades his whole system and comprises the entire psychic domain. Leibniz was aware of the whole but not of its laws.

Hume discarded, as did Spinoza, the role of contingency and chance in psychic life. For them even events that appear fortuitous are consequences of an iron law. Spinoza's view is experiential and mystic. For all practical purposes it is the renunciation of knowledge. But Hume's view is related to the Lockean genetic method, which shows the possibility of gradually, empirically coming to know the psychic world. Naturally, Hume paid a high scientific price for the first consistent psychological formulation of the genetic viewpoint—just as later Darwin's immediate successors had to pay dearly for the first formulation of the biogenetic law.

The price was the consequent one-sided interpretation of the psychic process:

. . . what we call a *mind*, is nothing but a heap or collection of different perceptions, united together by certain relations, and suppos'd, tho' falsely, to be endow'd with a perfect simplicity and identity [(17) I, 4, 2, p. 207].

When I enter most intimately into what I call *myself*, I always stumble on some particular perception. When my perceptions are removed for any time, as by sound sleep, so long am I insensible of *myself*, and may truly be said not to exist [(17) I, 4, 6, p. 252].

The latter quotation shows that Hume found it hard to make this sacrifice. For the assertion that the self can never be discerned without perceptions still leaves the possibility that the mind is more than perceptions—without which, however, it cannot be discerned.

The polemic around Hume also shows that that renunciation was not easily made. Lipps (Hume's German editor and commentator) and Cassirer tried to demonstrate that Hume was cognizant of connections that do not become habits, of associations; this obviously means that the mind consists of more than perceptions and their associational mechanism. "For Hume it is impossible that such similarity and comparability should be the basis of an association" (Lipps, 28th *Note* to the *Treatise*).

Cassirer ([1] I, p. 281) expressed a similar conviction. We believe that Lipps and Cassirer rightly focused attention on this point in Hume's system. Undoubtedly, the *Treatise* contains many elements overstepping the boundaries of mechanism. This is one of his great epistemological merits: "This uniting principle among ideas is not . . . an inseparable connection . . . nor yet are we to conclude that without it the mind cannot join two ideas . . . we are only to regard it as a gentle force." ([17] I, 1, 4, p. 10).

But if we compare these views with the tone of the *Enquiry*, which is experiential and less systematized— and even loosens the system—we reach a sharp contradiction. This contradiction shows that Hume, although distinctly led by law-making intentions, based much on personal experience and in his heart strongly resisted the dogmatism that followed from the inner logic of this law-making effort: "To me, there appear to be only three principles of connection among ideas, namely, *resem-*

blance, contiguity in time or place, and *cause* or *effect"* ([18] 3, p. 59). This thesis faithfully represents the spirit of his later works (for example, *On Passions*, II, 3). Here the system is unified and closed, and it eradicates—with the consistency of an established law—every experiential datum that would point in a different direction.

It may be stated, then, that both the "impression-idea" formula and the contradiction between *Treatise* and *Enquiry* reflect the effort of formulating a universal psychic law. I wish to elucidate Hume's conception with a few more appropriate quotations:

> . . . moralists have recommended as a . . . method of becoming acquainted with our own hearts . . . to recollect our dreams . . . In like manner . . . there might be . . . discoveries made from . . . ancient philosophy concerning *substances* . . . which . . . have a very intimate connection with the principles of human nature [(17) I, 4, 3, p. 219].

> And even in our wildest and most wandering reveries, nay in our very dreams, we shall find, if we reflect, that the imagination ran not altogether at adventures, but that there was still a connection upheld among the different ideas, which succeeded each other . . . a proof that the simple ideas . . . were bound together by some universal principle . . . [(18) 3, p. 596].

> Would you know the sentiments, inclinations, and course of life of the Greeks and Romans? Study well the temper and actions of the French and English [(18) 8, 1, p. 635].

All of us are subject to a unified psychic law: **Greeks, Romans, Frenchmen, Englishmen** alike. The structure of language, fancies, dreams, poetic imagination, visions, all come under the same unified psychic law. *The associative law has, through this atomization, brought mental life under a unified law and has traced all ideas back to their ultimate components, the impressions.*

IV

We are now in a position to outline Hume's associational mechanism. Alongside the mechanistic tendencies, I shall try to point out also those essential elements which overstep the proper limits of mechanism.

1. "The qualities, from which this association arises, and by which the mind is, after this manner, conveyed from one idea to another, are three, viz. *resemblance, contiguity* in time or place, and *cause* and *effect*" ([17], I, 1, 4, p. 11). Historically, the three associative factors differ in origin. Of the first, similarity, we have found traces in Bacon's theory; it became generally accepted only by Locke and his successors. The second, contiguity, we have found in every philosopher's doctrine since Bacon, although in widely divergent forms. But adding causality here is Hume's own idea and finds its only analogy in Spinoza.

According to Hume, then, it is similar impressions, spatially or temporally connected impressions, or impressions related as cause and effect that give rise to one another. This is the association mechanism in crystallized form. We have met the concept of this mechanism in the course of our investigations. We shall now examine this concept. The essence of this mechanistic doctrine is that one concept gives rise to another as though the recall of the second were inherent in the nature of the first. But we may interpret this mechanism also as serving a merely descriptive purpose insofar as it states that notions having given relationships with one another often succeed one another. The force giving rise to the association is nowhere.

We must emphasize that among the factors producing associations contiguity and causality appear side by side. This gives one pause, since in the sequel Hume traced causality back exactly to contiguity (coexistence and succession). In view of this fact, it might seem sufficient to mention only contiguity. But in the *Treatise* ([17] I, 4, 2, pp. 200 ff.). Hume points out that, in order to recognize a causal relationship, one does not necessarily have to remember preceding experiential incidents. Thus causality, independently of experiential factors or contiguity, may attain to existence, regularity, and an independent binding power; and precisely for this reason it can remain an independent factor alongside its creator, contiguity.

The idea of the parallel existence of cause and effect pervades the system of Hume. The parallel appearance of causality and contiguity has yet another significance. It was difficult for Hume to renounce the intrinsic law of reality, causality, and to dissolve it entirely into contiguity—as difficult as it was to dissolve intrinsic psychic law into the perceptions.

2. We have reviewed, then, the factors producing association, their historical origin and mechanical nature. We have yet to pose the question whether Hume viewed the associative—that is, the psychic—process as mechanical. This question came up already in connection with Locke, and there the answer was negative. Antimechanis-

tic elements have repeatedly been pointed out in Hume's philosophy. But our question can be decisively answered only by an elucidation of the whole scope of the concept of mechanism, since the specific notion of associational mechanism showed Hume's associative factors to be pure mechanism.

We call mechanism the course of those events—whether physical, biological, or historical—in which the succession of changes can come about in just one way; which, in other words, possesses only one degree of freedom. Change can come about here only in a well defined sequence of steps, each giving rise to the next, as in a machine. In such processes the motive forces (dynamism) are hidden. The machine either works or does not. Such a system is free of the influence of new forces that could modify the process. Classical Newtonian physics and every science that developed under its influence took this process as a model in its conception about any given process. The evolution of chemistry, the discovery of the chemical law of mass effect, the discovery of the dynamic equilibrium of concentrates, led far beyond this mechanical conception. It turned out that those processes and forces are not isolated; each process, qualitatively as well as quantitatively, in its course as well as in its outcome, is determined by the balance of all forces present. Scientists studied processes possessing several degrees of freedom, whose course is not strictly prescribed; these are the ones whose course varies, perhaps even infinitely. Processes possessing (denumerably or indenumerably many) infinite degrees of freedom are called dynamic. In these, equilibrium of the initial and final positions is determined by that of the prevailing conditions. Thus there are infinitely many degrees of freedom, or possible courses, of the event even though the specifications prescribe certain limits. According to investigations by Köhler and Wertheimer, psychic processes also show a dynamic "self-regulating" principle; here too the environment determines the course of events. From this, these researchers endeavored to draw inferences about the nature of physicochemical processes taking place in the nervous system. The conditions of a similar dynamic balance were examined by Lewin in his treatise, *Reward and Punishment*.

Taking all this into consideration, it is evident that, of those examined so far, Hobbes' concept of association was the classical mechanistic one. There each concept gave rise to the next in the order of previous occurrence. Everything in which this order could not be traced was accounted chaotic and outside the realm of lawful psychic events, for it was not mechanistically explainable, and Hobbes knew nothing of a dynamic interpretation. Descartes' conception was also mechanistic. The motion of vital forces mechanically gives rise to concepts but since, owing to the free movement of vital forces, this mechanism is blind, it gives birth to errors and is the cause of all deception.

Hume refrained from experimenting with any such physiological explanations. Concerning the association of ideas he said: "Its effects are everywhere conspicuous; but as to its causes, they are mostly unknown, and must be resolved into *original* qualities of human nature, which I pretend not to explain ([17] I, 1, 4, p. 13). He justified this stand with the argument that the scholar's task is to ascribe his observations to a minimum number of causes and to stop whenever he is in danger of pursuing obscure and uncertain speculations. Hume considered these three associational factors to be the ultimate psychic data. He could only conceive of their further examination in the analysis of the original traits of human nature; that is, in an anthropological-physiological investigation. But he kept aloof from such attempts. Hume never speculated about the "spirit" (life-force), which often appeared even in Locke's work. With this he avoided drawing the final conclusions from the mechanistic doctrine. A physiological interpretation of the three factors of association would have rendered his system an absolute mechanism. Instead, in accordance with the epistemological character of his philosophy, he endowed the psychical with independent existence. The implication is that it is not useful for new sciences to try to trace the subject matter of their investigations back to another science serving as a basis, before the laws governing the former are known.

Hume states clearly that the cause of associative connections is unknown. He was not open to physiological theorizing. Thus he left the door open for dynamic features in his theory, despite the mechanical nature of his three associational factors which we examine next.

3. He posits ". . . the liberty of the imagination to transpose and change its ideas" ([17], I, 1, 3, p. 10).

That we may understand the full extent of these relations, we must consider, that two objects are connected together in the imagination, not only when the one is immediately resembling, contiguous to, or the cause of the other, but also when there is interposed betwixt them a third object, which bears to both of them any of these relations [(17) I, 1, 4, p. 11].

Of all relations, that of resemblance is in this respect the most efficacious; and that because it not only causes an association of ideas, but also of dispositions, and makes us conceive the one idea by an act or operation of the mind, similar to that by which we conceive the other. This circumstance I have observed to be of great moment; and we establish it for a general rule that whatever ideas place the mind in the same disposition or in similar ones, are very apt to be confounded [(17) I, 4, 2, pp. 202–203].

There is indeed a principle of union among ideas, which at first sight may be esteemed different from any of these, but will be found at the bottom to depend on the same origin. When every individual of any species of objects is found by experience to be constantly united with an individual of another species, the appearance of any new individual of either species naturally conveys the thought to its usual attendant [(17) I, 3, 6, p. 93].

The insights contained in these passages widen the scope of association. These extensions blur the unequivocality of the mechanism built upon the three factors (resemblance, contiguity, causality). Mechanism is replaced by a complex overlapping system of relationships. In the final analysis, everything may be related to anything in this augmented association concept. We have a network of interconnected relationships before us, admitting of a large number of degrees of freedom, which shatters the boundaries of the mechanistic system. The originally unequivocal law based on the three associational factors here threatens to become chaotic unless the nature of dynamic self-regulation, the interplay and equilibrium of forces determining the various forms of association and their respective laws contained in the unity of psychic life and making for knowledge, are clarified.

4. There are however further elements in Hume's teaching that lead beyond the mechanism of the three basic associational factors.

We have already taken notice of certain relations, which make us pass from one object to another, even though there be no reason to determine us to that transition; and this we may establish for a general rule, that wherever the mind constantly and uniformly makes a transition without any reason, it is influenced by these relations [(17) I, 3, 6, p. 92].

Here, then, he juxtaposes the concept of rational motive and an entirely universal concept of associative mechanism. Clearly, the former falls outside the framework of mechanism. In another part of Hume's philosophy he states that reason has a proper function independent of mechanism. It concerns "conceptual discrimination," which is the direct continuation of the Molineaux problem examined by Locke, Leibniz, and Berkeley: the problem of concept formation.

Hume postulated that every concept that differs from another may be separated from it. On this basis, he demonstrated—following in Berkeley's footsteps—that abstract ideas are produced by the joining of similar particulars under the same name; that is to say, they are appearances created by associations. In this context he encountered Molineaux's problem and formulated it in the following way: Are the sphere and the color of the sphere two distinct concepts? Are these concepts altogether separable? He called this question the problem of the "distinction of reason," the problem of conceptual distinction, and generalized the question thus: "Of this kind is the distinction betwixt figure and the body figured; motion and the body moved" ([17] I, 1, 7, p. 24). This new question is synonymous with that of the connection between form of appearance and the bearer thereof.

The examination of the essence of the distinction of reason contributes two important factors to the understanding of Hume's philosophical thought.

It will appear from a further discussion of Hume's system that for him the phenomenon (form of appearance) was of the essence. This is produced by the three associational factors and necessarily follows from the functional nature of the human mind. The bearer of the phenomenon is only a semblance—an offspring of associations produced by the similarity of phenomena—and thus presupposes the phenomenon. The "distinction of reason" differentiates between the results of two associational processes. Essentially it is the cross of two associational processes whereby the various elements of an object become associated with different sets of objects and are thus separated. Unless we want to seek a contradiction in that the "distinction of reason" was an independent function for Hume, we have to conclude that he regarded the mind as an independent substance after all, although otherwise he treated it as a collection of associated perceptions. Here we again encounter an epistemological characteristic already emphasized: on the one hand the impression-idea formula dominates the mind; on the other hand the mind consists of perceptions connected by associations and is perhaps a product of them—yet this *product* possesses independent activity, separate from its origin. Hume attributed to them independent existence and power of judgement, that is, the ability to divide. Of course, this again overstepped the mechanistic theory.

About the distinction of reason, he wrote:

> ... the mind would never have dreamed of distinguishing a figure from the body figured, as being in reality neither distinguishable, nor different ... Thus, when a globe of white marble is presented, we receive only the impression of a white colour disposed in a certain form, nor are we able to separate and distinguish the colour from the form. But observing afterwards a globe of black marble and a cube of white, and comparing them with our former object, we find two separate resemblances, in what formerly seemed, and really is, perfectly inseparable ... We ... distinguish the figure from the colour by *a distinction of reason* ... we consider the figure and colour together ... but still view them in different aspects, according to the resemblances of which they are susceptible ... A person who desires us to consider the figure without thinking on its colour desires an impossibility [(17) I, 1, 7, p. 25].

There is a striking resemblance here between this "distinction of reason" and Locke's theory of concept formation. In the spirit of Hume's thought, we might say that objects of the same color or shape are associatively so closely connected that transition from one to the other is very easy. The easy transition between resembling phenomena lends the similarity of appearance—the very instruments and creators of associations which produce easy transitions—gives it a semblance of independent existence and thus "differentiates" it from the bearer of that form. But Hume failed to draw this inference, however well it would have suited his mechanistic system. On this issue too he kept his system away from ultimate mechanization.

5. Before investigating the traces of associational dynamism recognizable in Hume, we shall have to refer to one more consequence of his associational mechanics.

According to Hume, the certainty of connections produced by associations and our faith in them do not have the nature of independent experience. This kind of probability could not arise "unless the fancy melted together all those images that concur, and extracted from them one single idea or image, which is intense and lively in proportion to the number of experiments from which it is derived, and their superiority above their antagonists ([17] I, 3, 12, p. 140). According to this, affirmation, belief, and generally the various kinds of judgement prove to be associative products. At first glance this result seems to be an organic part of the mechanistic conception. But examined more closely, it appears that from quantitative changes in repetitions, there result qualitative changes in judgement-experiences depending on them. The shifting of quantitative changes to qualitative ones in itself presupposes a balance of forces behind the process. And the shift in the balance results in qualitative change in the experience. These and similar considerations lead us again beyond mechanics.

But this issue has great significance with regard to mechanism. The question of the power of associations is posed here methodically for the first time in the conceptual history of associations. This is the starting point of the examination of the power of associations which, under the term "associative equivalence" and beginning with Ebinghaus, became the most important instrument in associational investigation and the core of disputes storming around it.

The following quotations raise the problem of the time-induced fading of impressions.

. . . the difference between [memory] and the imagination lies in its superior force and vivacity [(17) I, 3, 5, p. 85].

And as an idea of the memory, by losing its force and vivacity, may degenerate to such a degree, as to be taken for an idea of the imagination; so, on the other hand, an idea of the imagination may acquire such a force and vivacity, as to pass for an idea of the memory, and counterfeit its effects on the belief and judgement [(17) I, 3, 5, p. 86].

Respective researches in modern psychology (Köhler, Wulf) have shown that behind the problem of blurring a dynamism is hidden such as we have pointed out in connection with the qualitative changes in experience that accompany quantitative changes in associations.

V

Now we may broach the subject of self-regulatory activities in the associational dynamism.

The question is: What is the systematizing agent in that intricate mass of associations that Hume rests on his three basic associative factors?

New associational relations had been added to the mechanism built on the original three basic associational elements. In consequence, the unequivocal mechanism of associations broke down. Their coordination is no longer conceivable on mechanistic grounds and thus they are best suited for the *description* of psychic phenomena but not for supplying their laws. Such a situation has often arisen in the history of the natural sciences. Such was the case, for instance, at the end of the last century in the age of the classical nominalistic analysis of Kirchoff, Helmholtz, etc. The mechanical connections between phenomena were clear. Phenomena are always connected by mechanisms. But Kirchoff's time was still unaware of a dynamism, an energetics, to explain the whole, to eliminate the contradictions and to coordinate the formulas of mechanics. Changes of form due to the equilibria peculiar to dynamics and energy, where every phase corresponds to an isolated group of mechanisms, were still unknown. An uncoordinated group of mechanisms can be held together only by a general dynamics in which quantitative changes produce qualitative modifications whose form is just the sought-for uncoordinated mechanism, thereby uniting these mechanisms by a law; these changes of quality or form being produced by the deployment of an equal quantity of energy. In physics this was accomplished at the beginning of this century by quantum theory and relativity theory.

We found such guiding forces earlier in our investigation. In almost every system we have examined, the basic fact emerged that the direction of our interests, material and intellectual, exercises a decisive influence upon the creation of our associations. But these systems did not transcend the boundaries of mere experience. Hume far surpassed them, but even he did not discover a general dynamics.

> There is implanted in the human mind a perception of pain and pleasure . . . But pain and pleasure have two ways of making their appearance in the mind . . . either [as] in impression to the actual feeling, or only in idea . . . the influence of these upon our actions is far from being equal. Impressions always actuate the soul, but 'tis every idea which has the same effect . . . Did impressions alone influence the will, we should every moment of our lives be subject to the greatest calamities; because . . . we should not be provided by nature with any principle of action, which might impel us to avoid them. On the other hand, did every idea influence our actions, our condition could not be much mended. For such is the unsteadiness and activity of thought, that the images of every thing, especially of goods and evils, are always wandering in the mind . . . It would never enjoy a moment's peace. . . . Nature has therefore chosen a medium . . . The effect then of belief is to raise up a simple idea to an equality with our impressions, and bestow on it a like influence on the passions. This effect it can only have by making an idea approach an impression in force and vivacity [(17) I, 3, 10, pp. 118–119].

Faith, then, deriving from the frequency of the connection of concepts, supplies the latter their strength. Associations of concepts of various strengths, impressions of varying strength vie with each other so as to prevail in men in the form of thoughts, to gain influence in forming judgement. The full significance of Hume's conception is shown by a few analogies. (

In Hume's empiricism, the utilitarianism of English philosophy presents itself. In this point Hume is superior to the empiricist-sensualist Locke, who cannot find in the psychic activity the elements of compliance with reality and consequently makes practice the direct criterion of reality, of the difference between reality and dream.

We may find some interesting analogies in present-day psychology with Hume's concepts, which he endows with the strength of impressions: the *"Signal-Handlungen"* of the well known ornithologist Lorenz, and Lewin's *"Aufforderungs-Charaktere"* are also conditions calling to action to give meaning to some impression.

Bühler (*Geistige Entwicklung des Kindes,* p. 434) sees man's superiority over the animals in that he is able to try out his potentially harmful acts as experiments at his desk, in his head. And this is extremely close to Hume's idea that concepts have the power of impressions.

In the chaos of associations, the basis for creating a dynamics, a regulating system, is the will to live, to survive; its contradictory factors produce the play of forces which selects and brings to the surface adequate associations.

Yet Hume's was admittedly a bungling attempt. His results were rendered abortive by Hume himself, as witness his remarks to the effect that the essential difference between concepts and impressions is in their respective strengths. By this the factor harboring the possibility of self-regulation is made subject to his mechanical explanation. For self-regulation, here as elsewhere, may only be found in the play of forces of opposing factors in their dynamic equilibrium. The two poles are supplied by Hume: the duality of concept and impression. Vital force moves between them. Yet the motive force is not clear. It ought to be the immanent power of the two poles. We can find traces of this in Hume's *On Passions*, but the conception there is not brought to a common denominator with this even in terminology.

Man is not moved by interest alone or passion alone, but by the struggle in him of both [(18′) 4, 7].

...reason ... the judgement of truth and falsehood ... can never ... be any motive to the will ... but so far as it touches some passion or affection ... What is commonly ... called reason ... is ... a calm passion ... [(18′) 4, 1–2].

Yet, generally speaking, affectivity is not immanent in concept and impression, but plays the part of the third, regulated, factor in Hume's system.

These beginnings are built on by Freud and Lewin in modern psychology. That Hume could not have reached this conclusion becomes clear in the following interesting remark: ". . . it is evident that [the senses] . . . are incapable of giving rise to the notion of the continu'd existence of their objects, after they no longer appear to the senses" ([17] I, 4, 2, p. 188).

Here we have reached the outer limit of Hume's psychology. For him, the unconscious lies outside of the reach of science—properly speaking, it does not exist. It is evident from this that Hume could not recognize those dynamic factors not in the consciousness. This is why he had to leave the structure of dynamism unfinished, even though his insights probed into its very core.

VI

We have endeavored to outline Hume's associational mechanism and the visible traces of dynamism. Now our task is to shed light on the genesis of the six basic cognitive concepts already referred to. Hume turns to the mechanical explanation, trying to trace the basic concepts to associational mechanisms.

1. Hume follows Berkeley when he demonstrates by a multitude of examples that we have no impressions of our abstract ideas. The essence of his argument is this: we cannot perceive abstractions with our senses; so abstractions must derive from self-perception. But self-perception supplies us only with affections and emotional effects. Consequently, such concepts as substance, space, time, object, self, causality, may only present themselves in the imagination ([17] I, 1, 7, pp. 17 ff.).

Subsequently he examines how these can be produced in the imagination.

Substance and its modes are groups of simple concepts that, by common appearance in space and through habit, have become associated. Since, owing to their being associated, the imagination easily glides from one to the other, the semblance of a common denominator among them, termed "substance," came into existence. Hume says: as they occur together—or if they do not the occurrence of one gives rise to the rest—it is patent why habit refers them to an unknown bearer. To the latter we usually assign a name; by aid of this name we recall the aggregate of concepts and the illusion of substance is created.

The traits that we become acquainted with only later are fitted into that aggregate through new associative connections and thus broaden the concept of substance.

About the concepts of time and space, Hume wrote: "As 'tis from the disposition of visible and tangible objects we receive the idea of space, so, from the succession of ideas and impressions we form the idea of time; nor is it possible for time alone ever to make its appearance or be taken notice of by the mind" ([17] I, 2, 3, p. 35). By the method he used in examining substance and its modes he demonstrates that these concepts could be produced only in the imagination.

The concepts of space and time are both appearances produced by associative connections. In Hume's sense the question whether time or space exist would be meaningless. By this he avoids Berkeley's confusion and escapes the necessity to deny the existence of all being besides God and the self. In his formulation, the question is not whether there is such a thing as time or space. He turns the problem around and asks "why we suppose them to have an existence *distinct* from the mind and perception" ([17] I, 4, 2, p. 188).

In the dialectic antithesis between the two poles, existence and nonexistence, he found the synthesis in the discovery of the law of psychic existence, and accordingly the entire epistemological enigma became a psychological question for him. By such a formulation of the question, he laid the foundation of criticism—not only the criticism of Kant, who regarded Hume as his direct spiritual predecessor (Prolegomena, Introduction), but also psychological criticism, still in an embryonic stage but rendered possible by modern developmental psychology.

2. Hume approached the subjects of object-constancy

and personal identity the same way. He demonstrated that the object is not constant, not permanently existent for the mind, but a mass of intermittent, emerging and submerging impressions and concepts. Nor is the personality an identically existing entity but a conglomeration of variable perceptions ([17] I, 4, 2, pp. 19 ff, 206 ff). For him, object-constancy and personal identity are but the filling out of cognitive gaps by postulating a durable existence. This postulate is produced by those associations that originate among the bits and pieces of perceptions. These associations necessarily induce our cognition to jump from one such fragment to the other. As a necessary result of the transition, there arises a semblance, a notion, of identity of the personality and of objects. The strength of the belief in these semblances, the self-evident and deeply rooted nature of the concepts of identity and constancy, are due to the fact that the associations involved are associations of resemblance which involve, according to Hume, not only the concepts but also the dispositions producing them. The consequences of his viewpoint are summed up in the following passages: "The idea of motion [to him identical with temporal succession] . . . must resolve itself into the idea of extension . . . of solidity . . ." ([17] I, 4, 4, p. 228); ". . . solidity or impenetrability is nothing, but an impossibility of annihilation" (*ibid.*, p. 229). And since he demonstrated that the impression of solidity is gained exclusively by sensory qualities, "when we exclude these sensible qualities, there remains nothing in the universe which has such an existence" (*ibid.*, p. 231).

Hume thus succeeded in reducing, by aid of associations, every basic cognitive form or substratum to the sensory experience of solidity. But here he reached the bounds of his system. For all the firm logic his mechanical system of associations had been built up with, the foundation, the associated element, remained the sensory impression. Its rationalization, its exclusion from the realm of science, both show the inner contradiction of the mechanistic conception.

Hume's age did not possess the means to resolve this contradiction. Hume honestly admits of and lets stand the contradiction, keeping what results he was able to obtain: the outward appearance of phenomena, the associative mechanism which produce its outer garb. Hume's criticism is helpless when it comes to the basic problem of psychology. He points out the contradiction but finds no way out. This was recognized also by Cassirer ([1] II, p. 226).

3. The problem of causality remains to be dealt with. Naturally the *Treatise* does not ask for the existing connections in nature. The problem is formulated as before: Why do we see natural processes the way they appear in the light of causality?

But at this point the question is asked in its most decisive and momentous context. Criticism now has to furnish proof of its own *raison d'être*, its truth value. For even if we can clarify the psychic reason why we see things in causal connection, we still have to ask how this viewpoint furnishes the foundation of the prognosis, by which it is also justified.

Here again Hume offers a combination of two elements. The *Treatise* is imbued with critical spirit. But here the principle of evenness in the processes of nature, a heritage of Berkeley, presents itself. In the *Enquiry* it becomes the ruling principle, laying the foundation for the mechanical associative concept of causality. Hume's

internal struggle took place between these two intellectual poles, and their reconciliation was the inner purpose
of the *Treatise.*

This is the essence of causality according to Hume:

. . . of those relations, which depend not upon the
mere ideas . . . one can be trac'd beyond our senses . . .
causation [(17) I, 3, 2, p. 74].

. . . we have discovered a new relation betwixt cause
and effect . . . This relation is their *constant conjunc-
tion.* Contiguity and succession are not sufficient to
make us pronounce any two objects to be cause and
effect, unless we perceive that these two relations are
preserved in several instances [*Ibid.*, p. 87].

If reason determin'd us it wou'd proceed upon that
principle *that instances* of which we have had no experience, must resemble those of which we have had
experience, and that the course of nature continues
always uniformly the same [*Ibid.*, p. 89].

The two poles are thus seen together. On the one hand,
habit—for the first time—becomes a general principle of
knowledge. It is capable of connecting concepts so closely
that the appearance of a lawful regular connection is
created. On the other hand, the principle of the uniformity of the natural process makes its appearance,
inspired by reason. The first principle is critical-psycho-
logical; the second stems from empirium. In Hume, both
are tinged with a rationalistic hue. (Cf. Köhler, *Gestalt-
psychologie.*) Cassirer pointed out ([1] I, p. 261) that
Hume approached rationalism on this issue. A significant

difference between Hume and the rationalists lies in his psychological viewpoint, which stems from his empiricism. Between psychologism and rationalism the difference in general is the empirical character of the former. In rationalism a supposed autonomy of the mind is contrasted with empiricism, while in psychologism we witness the confrontation of two empirical strata, an inner and an outer one, which necessarily lead to criticism. The empirical origin of the other principle is rather evident. This is due to the experience of the uniformity mentioned above. We have seen, however, that for the author of the *Treatise* this principle can be founded only upon reason, upon consciousness possessing autonomous activity. Hume chose the associational structure of reason, proposing the principle of causality on the basis of habit. Associations and habit became a general principle of knowledge by the aid of which Hume formulated the interdependence of consciousness and nature.

If all the scenes of nature were continually shifted in such a manner that no two events bore any resemblance to each other, but every object was entirely new, without any similitude to whatever had been seen before, we should never, in that case, have attained the least idea of necessity, or of a connection among these objects. We might say, upon such a supposition, that one object or event has followed another; not that one was produced by the other. The relation of cause and effect must be utterly unknown to mankind. Inference and reasoning concerning the operations of nature would, from that moment, be at an end; and the memory and senses remain the only canals by which the knowledge of any real existence could possibly have access to the mind. Our ideas, therefore, of necessity and causation arise entirely from the uniformly observable in the operations of nature, where similar objects are constantly conjoined together, and the mind is determined by custom to infer the one from the appearance of the other [(18) 7, 1, p. 635].

After having thus clarified the problem of causality, Hume discusses the methods of discovering causal connection. These methods are reiterations of Bacon's *tabulae* in a more advanced age and by a thinker of wider perspective. The simultaneous appearance of the notion of *tabulae* and the principle of the regularity of nature show that Bacon's induction was enriched by new data regarding associations and epistemology. Here Hume supplies us with a formulation of induction of unparalleled clarity, lifting it out of a context where it was still burdened by scholastic notions ([10] 7).

After this Hume embarks, in connection with causality, on the analysis of the question of probability.

4. Contradictory experiences determine not causality but probability. Just as faith depended upon the strength of associations producing concepts, so now the probability of causes depends upon the strength of associations supporting the concept of causality in the face of contradictory associations ([17] I, 4, 2). By this, all arguments founded on reason are dissolved into probability because we do not know any connections that are unequivocal and without contrary connections, and consequently we do not find any that cover all future cases. There is no concept that would move our entire faith. Even inference

based on proof becomes a mere probability if there are many interpolated steps between starting point and end point ([17] 1, 3, 13, p. 144).

In the analysis of causality Hume's skepticism reaches its climax. It is immediately clear that this skepticism—which dissolves everything palpable into semblance, all causality into probability—is a direct and explicit result of associations. Here the connection between associations and skepticism does not require as profound an analysis as it did in Descartes. This shows clearly that to counterbalance skepticism the mechanism of associations had to become more and more rigid. Against skepticism, then, which follows from associations, the mechanism of associations is the refuge. As we have seen in Locke's case, associations harbor peril and rescue at the same time. It is a peculiar abode where—it appears—we must live and die.

It is important to refer the reader here to Windelband's opinion about Hume's skepticism.

Hume indeed denied the possibility of metaphysics. In this sense he was a veritable skeptic. But as far as mathematics is concerned he was not a skeptic but a rationalist. He was not one as regards experiential knowledge, because he held that so true and indubitable that sometimes we could almost call him a sensualist. He was skeptical, again, about the empirical *sciences*, insofar as these are held capable of proving interpretative causal principles beyond the facts. The correct name of this doctrine is empirical skepticism. And since Hume, like Comte and his disciples, thought that he could be content with the establishing of facts and their chronological order, and could manage without explanatory theories, he may be called a positivist in this sense. Thus Hume is the only and true father of positivism [(5) p. 346].

One of the roots of positivism, then, springs from the facts that associational connections and further theoretical reflections built on them do not contain natural certainty, and only the sensory impressions making up the basis of these connections may be regarded with certainty as conditions existing in nature. The psychogenesis of positivism is intimated here.

The emphasis on probabilities in Hume's system gives a quality to his skepticism peculiarly his own. By this he wanted to neutralize the famous argument which, beginning with Plato, had so often been leveled against skepticism. The essence of it is that skepticism, when doubting everything, exempts at least one thesis—namely, the one asserting the thesis. This is its contradiction. And if it does extend it to that thesis, it demolishes the doctrine itself. In this dilemma Hume chose a third way—probability. For him, it is not "true" and "false" that confront each other, but various degrees of empirical probability. This statement is in harmony with Windelband's above-quoted opinion, for Windelband branded Hume a skeptic only in regard to the tenets of metaphysics and the empirical sciences; that is to say, in regard to those sciences that aim to possess absolute knowledge.

Hume's skeptical analyses of space, time, and causality show numerous analogies with the findings of developmental psychology and psychoanalysis. Though we are still far from drawing the ultimate epistemological conclusions from the findings of developmental psychology, we might derive an important guide from expounding its most important results in order to illustrate Hume's analyses. But that would lead us beyond the scope of the present investigation.

VII

We have seen how Hume succeeded in tracing the basic data of cognition, by aid of associational connections, back to elementary impressions, and how he pointed out that these data are products of habit. By this analytical method, the quality of concepts became the quantitative measure of the strength of associations produced by the frequency of the constituent impressions. This connection is on the dividing line between mechanical and dynamic theories. On the one hand, it contains a summative connection which is mechanistic, and on the other hand from this summative connection new qualities—impression, faith, concept—arise which would correspond to dynamism and would not at all fit into a mechanistic pattern. Hume himself asked the question whether from the repetition of the same successions there may come at any time anything other than repetitive succession. Here we have caught a glimpse of a thread running through Hume's entire philosophy about which Hume himself, interrupting his train of thought, again and again wondered in expectant perplexity. This problem awaits solution.

Impression, concept, remembering, thinking, judged-as-being, fancy, judged-as-probable, faith, knowledge—these are the various qualities of the psychic process in Hume's terminology. His main goal was to explain them. Cognitive concepts, as we have seen, are likewise produced by the frequency of temporal and spatial juxta-position.

It appears that Hume perceived that his explanation contains difficulties, and we may infer that that was the reason why he emphasized the radical differences between qualities in experiences.

There is a great difference betwixt the simple conception of the existence of an object, and the belief of it, and as this difference lies not in the parts or composition of the idea which we conceive; it follows that it must lie in the *manner* in which we conceive it [(17) I, 3, 6, p. 94].

Such a quantitative explanation of qualities of experience remains a mere psychical atomism which cannot explain anything if the dynamism—in which these qualities are changes in form corresponding to changes in the distribution of energy—is absent. We see then that one finds in Hume both the mechanistic and the dynamic conceptions, not only in regard to the question of the essence of associations but also in regard to the complete structure of the psychical. He had not yet freed himself of the first, and he had not yet entirely perfected the other. Our picture of Hume will be even clearer if we emphasize two consequences of his doctrine:

1. All basic cognitive concepts and all our perceptions —that is to say, every event of the psychic realm (excepting impressions and knowledge)—may be produced as any one of the experiential qualities of the psyche; that is, as belief, concept, memory, thought, fantasy, the assigning of a measure of probability (to something), etc.

But there is an infinity of such experiential qualities, for example there are infinitely many degrees of probability, infinitely many transitions between categories of experience. The psychic process, then, takes place on an infinity of planes, the basic cognitive concepts may be of infinitely many kinds, on just as many levels of consciousness. Thus we face a psychic mechanism resembling Spinoza's infinity of attributes. Here too impression is the basis of all, since for Hume there is no idea without impression. In Spinoza's doctrine, the category of *res extensa* corresponds to this. Knowledge itself, which also appears to be an exception among the levels of the psychic process, is none other than the ultimate of the experience of probability for Hume; however, it is nearly unattainable.

2. Objects which by frequency of their contiguity constitute space, extensions which by the repetition of their succession produce the concepts of motion and time, are themselves semblances arisen through associative connections. Even the self, personal identity, which perceives all this is produced by associative connections, and there is no impression corresponding to it. Thus, the forms of knowledge are constructed by the permanent connection of a certain type of basic material which produces the next element, the other basic cognitive concept. Then the next one is created by the constant simultaneous appearance, through associations, of the two modes of this concept. Solidity gives rise to space, space to time, time to causation. But these overlap, exist simultaneously, side by side, and together, as was shown by developmental psychology. According to developmental psychology, the elements producing the forms of knowledge appear in the language, in dreams, in nervous and psychotic states, in the reasoning of primitives and of chil-

dren, taking the place of developed forms. The product and the basic element, its cause, coexist and overlap. The older and newer forms leading from the self to the object on the phylogenetic scale coexist and regressions and rudiments are all too frequent. Hume constructed only the mechanistic cross-section of this system of inter-dependences, which, however, is incipient in his doctrine as bequeathed to us in the *Treatise*. Naturally enough, his mechanistic bent was frustrated by that doubly inter-woven system of relations. Although the complex matrix of the web is still imbued with mechanistic notions, the fact of its complexity breaks through the framework of any mechanism.

In connection with the question of the dynamic self-regulation of associations, we pointed out that in Hume the mechanistic system is produced by the inadequacy of the construction of his dynamism of drives. We arrived at the same conclusion in the problem discussed under this heading. In Hume's theory, the bearer of quantitative changes, this substratum of the mind and its dynamics, is missing. *the unconscious*

VIII

Recent and historically antiquated forms, earlier and present evolutionary formations, coexist and mutually in-fluence each other in the psychic process and in cognition. The more primitive forms of consciousness are connected to more than the cognitive form corresponding to that stage. Each step on the phylogenetic road of human cog-nition—that is, of the process of evolution leading from the human self and its impulses to the objectification of things—is embedded in the evolutionary steps corresponding to the respective step of the human psyche. Furthermore, every step taken toward the objectification of a thing is based on earlier steps without which it does not exist and by which it is fitted into the evolutionary pattern. These phylogenetic steps are repeated in the ontogenetic process. For the individual, too, every next step is based upon these, which, in turn, are likewise embedded in the corresponding whole of the evolution of the psychic process, the latter itself having been built upon the earlier structure.

All these *coexist*; they do not care a fig for a mechanistic interpretation or for the accustomed arrangement into categories of space and time, and they frustrate all attempts at analogies even of space and time. The nervous system of the human organism; the central sympathetic and parasympathetic nervous system; the gradual cerebralization (Monakow) of functions; the endocrine secretional regularization and, lastly, the functions arising from nerve centers superimposed on one another with the coordination of the three nervous systems and the endocrine system—perhaps only these might serve as analogues. But this may be more than analogy.

The mechanistic element in Hume's construction consists in his effort to reduce everything to a single final basic principle. This effort is most suggestively expressed in the idea-impression formula. The dynamic element may be seen in the realization that, in Hume's system, we are faced with levels of consciousness built on top of each other, which mutually presuppose each other as constituents but not as *the* final identical basic constituent. Dynamism and mechanism lie that close to each other; yet the abyss gaping between the two is enormous!

Hume, then, was cognizant of new constructs created

by the piling up of identical elements. By this, he far outstripped the "psychology of ability" which could not conceive of abilities as being other than certain final attributes of the psyche. (Klemm, *Geschichte der Psychologie, Wissenschaft und Hypothese* series.) At the same time he reached beyond Kantian criticism here, for the *Anschauungen* of the latter are essentially the rudiments of abilities. For Hume, these forms were not a priori. In this, Hume anticipated Hegel's daring dialectics which dissolved the Kantian categories.

In Hume's system, the dynamic aspect of drives which we witnessed in Locke and Leibniz was not further developed. The new element in his doctrine was that while investigators had been trying to demonstrate the possibility of a unified psychic law, to him that was given. The effort of demonstrating that possibility left no chance to his predecessors to construct that law. Hume was the first to evolve a consistent unified system of the phenomenon of consciousness and with it of the cognitive process. From him the line of evolution of the epistemological influence of associations leads directly to Kant. Contemporary (eighteenth-century) associational psychology, so-called, created nothing new from an epistemological viewpoint. The only achievement of that school was the new formulation of a physiological problem, the problem of the physiological significance of associations. Owing to that significance, their discussion belongs in a review of the associational theories of physiological psychology.

Kant: The Transcendental Deduction of Categories

I

IN KANT'S SYSTEM, baroque philosophy—that golden age of Western philosophy—reached a climax. The findings of the natural sciences disclosed the outlines of the epistemological problem more and more clearly.

Scientific results became the public treasure of the age. But the question whether these results were not merely accidental could be answered only by solving the basic problem of epistemology. Understandably, in this its Saturnian age, philosophy, which previously had been dominated by ethical and theological considerations, is brought under the influence of epistemological questions. We have pointed out earlier that the history of the concept of association is a direct function of this epistemological influence, at times even its determiner.

Kant wrought a synthesis of the philosophy of his age. What that age had accomplished in empiricism, rationalism, and skeptical phenomenalism supplied him with the material he attempted to harmonize and to balance in the course of the development of his philosophy. Kantian criticism presents the closed, finished, and unequivocal

160 ·

examination and evaluation of the entire intellectual heritage of the various branches of philosophy that was built of the treasure of knowledge accessible to that epoch. This fact explains the depth and influence of that philosophy. It is at the same time an eloquent example of how any kind of attempt at a system in philosophy is based on the impact and width of knowledge that serve as the raw material and backdrop for the various schools of philosophy (empiricism, rationalism, etc.). And these directions apparently stem from differences in point of view.

The development of mathematics and its applicability impressed Kant as a decisive datum in favor of rationalism. He was also strongly influenced, as were Locke and Hume, by the empiricism of the natural sciences and even by historical, political, and psychological empiricism. In the midst of that contradiction, the question of being and consciousness was specified into the problem of the mathematical, rational, manageability of inductive-empirical findings. Without a doubt, this is the experiential basis of setting his problem and his goal, which in the *Critique* is formulated in the question, "how are a priori synthetic propositions possible?"

The sensualist-materialist and the sensualist-idealist clashes of his age also left a mark on Kant's philosophy. To the former he opposed the *"Ding-an-sich,"* to the latter the denial of idealism (*Analytics of Maxims*, 2, 4). As for sensualistic idealism, according to Kant, only sensory perception is in the realm of cognition; and just as in sensualistic materialism, in Kant's doctrine too the objectively existing external world is the cause of phenomena. Kant believed in the existence of such a thing, although he thought it unknowable "in itself."

After having thus examined the elements of this philosophy, we shall now focus our attention on its construction.

II

Hume demonstrated that the basic forms of cognition cannot be acquired empirically, these being appearances produced by associative, subjective connections. Hume's basic question was, why do we perceive these connections as causation, as a necessary connection? The epistemological problem here posited pervades Kant's entire system. When producing the synthesis of the philosophical systems of his age, he proceeds with this in mind, on the basis of Hume's original question. Kant's formulation of the question is: How is it possible that causation, although of subjective origin, possesses objective validity? Under Hume's influence, Kant was convinced of the subjective origin of causation. Therefore he started from there to examine the transcendental structure of subjectivity. The question of how the (according to Hume) purely empirical phenomenon of connection between cause and effect might possess general validity must have necessarily occurred to Kant, who was a disciple of Wolff's rationalistic school. That question, in the terminology of our own problem, may be formulated thus: How is it possible that associations, these subjective processes, become the constituents of the general law of nature? Or, more simply, how can associations produce causal cognition of universal validity?

Kant, then, unlike many of his predecessors, saw in associations not an element engendering confusion and obscurity but the means of acquiring true knowledge. Under the title *Apologie für die Sinnlichkeit,* he interpreted sensory illusions and denied the charge that sensation is illusory. Sensation and imagination supply us only with raw material. Should illusions arise, reason is to be blamed for its failure to interpret correctly the data received ([21] *Erste Anklage*, 9).

How is a priori synthetic judgement possible? Because of the controversies around it, this problem has to be explained. According to Kant, every judgement whose subject does not contain its predicate is synthetic. But since the subject contains just that which we have put into it *per definicionem*, it has been doubtful from the beginning which judgements are analytical and which synthetic. Thus according to Couturat: "Since a science can be deduced from a system of axioms with purely analytical judgements, we may limit the domain of synthetic a priori judgements to the axioms." But from our point of view it is clear that the question of the possibility of a priori synthetic propositions is identical with the question of how propositions of general validity may come about through associations. These latter acquire logical form by the purely formal linking of subject and predicate. In that case, subject and predicate are not connected to each other by language, that is, by human history or covenant, but only by a generalization of empirically ascertained coexistence, while the linguistic relationship used to express that generalization or that coexistence is in no way discoverable. We shall learn Kant's view of associations by following his proof of the possibility of a priori synthetic judgement.

III

Kant's final answer may be summarized very simply: Time and space, as pure forms of intuition, and the 12 a priori concepts of the table of categories, are attributes of man's subjective nature (that is, of the transcendental subjectum) without which knowledge and even sense perception and sensation are impossible. The objects, phenomena, and relations given empirically could become objects, phenomena, and relations only through a priori concepts and pure intuition. The possibility of a priori synthetic propositions is given in the fact that these are brought about by intuitions and categories, that is to say, a priori they precede all experience. They acquire their validity by the fact that all later experience is possible only through intuitions and categories and thus necessarily contains the principle of the same synthesis. Their a priori nature comes from their having arisen according to a priori given and not empirically acquired laws of reason and intuition. Finally, the reason for their synthetic nature is that empirically we do not find a connection between their subjects and predicates; that connection can be uncovered only by transcendental analysis, from which it follows that it is produced by pure intuitions and a priori concepts.

Kant found 12 categories and two pure intuitions, that is, 14 levels about which he could assert that the connections produced by them are not accidental but have general validity. These levels are, on the one hand, space and time, on the other hand unity, plurality, totality, reality, negation, limitation, substance-and-accident, cause-and-effect, reciprocity, possibility-impossibility, existence-nonexistence, necessity. These, besides insuring general validity, embrace the whole realm of knowledge. Only they render things intelligible and thus, by virtue of the connections established through them, *reason bestows law on the universe*. Everything that we have recognized in our experience and in phenomena as regular and general has been bestowed on them by pure a priori concepts and forms of pure intuition, because without this synthesis that which is "manifold" would be purely accidental.

With this, the part played by associations in intellectual cognition is rescued; their validity is explained but at the price of abandoning the objective world, the laws of the "*noumenon*," Kant recognized associations arising outside of these levels ([21, loc. cit.]). These he held attributable to the activity of the imagination. The existence of these prompted him to answer Hume's question by introducing the labeling method of categories and thus to explain the secret of *validity*. Essentially, he expressed the movement of the "manifold" on the levels of categories (which are in many ways identical with Hume's planes of psychological phenomena), that is to say, on the various evolutionary stages of the sense of reality. But these levels, the categories, are worth our consideration in themselves. Upon closer examination it appears evident that their ancestors are to be found in Hume's qualities of the psychic process. This is best seen in the groups of categories quality and modality, reality, negation, limitation, possibility, existence, and necessity. And to find the analogy with Hume we need only add to the opposites of the last three of these that "concepts are experienced as reality, as negation, etc." The third set of categories—object, causation, and personal identity—contains this form of knowing. The categories of the fourth group are also among the conditions of the production of our usual associations in everyday experience. Undoubtedly, this arrangement of associations contains a certain element of arbitrariness. Kant's commentators have pointed this out on repeated occasions. We shall deal with the origin and significance of this arbitrariness in connection with Lange's views on this subject.

But first we shall have to examine in general how connecting and association take place on these levels; that is, how experiences and along with them a priori synthetic propositions arise.

IV

Kant employed transcendental deduction to show how categories are introduced into the empirical. For this purpose, he analyzed the cognitive process. According to him, the process of cognition takes place as follows:

Whatever the origin of our representations may be . . . as modifications of the mind they must always belong to the internal sense and . . . must therefore finally be subject to the formal condition of that internal sense, namely time, in which they are all arranged, joined, and brought into certain relations to each other . . . In order to change this manifold into a unity of intuition . . . it is necessary first to run through the manifold and then to hold it together. It is this act which I call the synthesis of apprehension . . . [(19) **1, 2, 2**, paragraph 1].

Thus, already the activity of the sense organs produces a synthesis, a connection. "The sense knows the phenomenon in the perception, empirically" (*ibid.*). The sense-produced synthesis of apprehension is accordingly the first stage where the "manifold" becomes imbued with the nature and mode of activity of the subject. The synthesis thus created serves as a datum for reproduction or association.

We need not outline here again the function of association or reproduction. Kant means the same by it as does English associational psychology. He surpasses it when he points out: "This law of reproduction, however, presupposes that the phenomena themselves are really subject to such a rule and that there is in the variety of these representations a system of concomitancy subject to certain rules . . ." (*ibid.*, paragraph 2).

Associations are produced by empirical imagination in the reproduction, but the latter presupposes the existence of duplications in the material that presents itself to the person. While in Hume's doctrine this repetition meant the principle of regularity in the processes of nature, which he inherited from Berkeley, Kant ascribes it to the synthesis produced in apprehension, and concludes:

> The synthesis of apprehension is thus inseparably connected with the synthesis of reproduction; and since the latter is the transcendental basis of the possibility of all knowledge in general, the productive synthesis of the imagination is the transcendental capacity of the imagination [*ibid.*].

Thus was the substance of recognition occasioned. Kant characterized recognition as follows: "Without our being conscious that what we are thinking now is the same as what we thought a moment before, all reproduction in the series of representations would be in vain" (*ibid.*, paragraph 3). And this consciousness stems from the function of recognition. Recognition is produced by apperception, which ". . . cannot be anything but the formal unity of our consciousness in the synthesis of the manifold in our representations" (*ibid.*).

There are, then, three stages in cognition; i.e., there are three subjective sources of knowledge: sense organ, imagination, and apperception. But it turns out that apperception is presupposed in all and the synthesis of both reproduction and apprehension fit into the unity of apperception. That is necessary, for apperception is the consciousness of the unity of the self, and according to Kant: "No knowledge can take place in us . . . without . . . unity of consciousness. . . ." (*ibid.*).

Kant saw the birth of knowledge as follows:

The first that is given us is the *phenomenon* . . . As every phenomenon contains a manifold and . . . perceptions are found in the mind singly and scattered, a connection of them is necessary such as they cannot have in the senses by themselves. There exists therefore in us an active power for the synthesis of the manifold, which we call imagination, and the function of which, as applied to perceptions, I call apprehension. . . . It must be clear, however, that even this apprehension of the manifold could not alone produce a coherence of impressions or an image, without some subjective power of coupling one perception . . . to another. . . . It is necessary therefore that their reproduction should be subject to a rule, by which one representation connects itself . . . with a second and not with a third. It is this subjective and empirical ground of reproduction according to rules, which is called the *association* of representations. If this unity of association did not possess an objective foundation also . . . it

would be a mere accident that phenomena lend themselves to a certain connection in human knowledge. . . .
This objective ground of all association of phenomena
I call their *affinity*, and this can nowhere be found
except in the principle of the unity of apperception
applied to all knowledge which is to belong to me"
[(19) 1, 2, 3].

In sum, the imagination also takes part in the synthesis
of apprehension, and does this by virtue of association,
which connects the "manifold" on the basis of experiential simultaneity. But the associative influence of the
imagination could also give rise to accidental connections, had it not another determining factor which pre-
cedes experience and objectively determines the direction
of associations: this is called affinity. Above we have attempted to compare Kant and Hume in relation to the
genesis of associations. Here the difference is sharpened.
In Hume, the uniformity of a process in nature is the
basis of associations and the concept of causation and
validity produced by them. In Kant the empirical basis
of repetition is the synthesis of apprehension, which,
according to the passage quoted, entertains a mutually
determining relationship with the subjective phenomenon
of association. The common basis to these is not the
uniform process of nature but the transcendental affinity
discoverable in apperception—for in Kant the law rests
not with the *noumenon* but with the spirit. This is the
transcendental principle of the self, the unity of personality and experience. But:

This unity of apperception with reference to the synthesis of imagination is the *understanding*, and the

same unity with reference to the transcendental synthesis of the imagination, the *pure understanding*. It must be admitted therefore that there exist in the understanding pure forms of knowledge *a priori* which contain the necessary unity of the pure synthesis of the imagination in reference to all possible phenomena. These are the categories, that is, the pure concepts of the understanding [*ibid.*].

This is the final result of transcendental deduction. Now it is plain in what way empirical knowledge contains a cognitive element, that is, how categories are introduced into experience. In Kant's words, "how a priori synthetic propositions are possible."

V

Transcendental deduction has shown that Kant broke up the concept of association into several overlapping concepts or functions. He pointed out that without inner regulating principles associations would connect everything to everything else and would not obey any rule, system, or law.

With this, the concept of association is deepened. In place of the hastily etched contours and many confusions of the general concept of association, there is now the nicely elaborated system of apprehension, recognition, and reproduction. In connection with this, the generalized concept of psyche is differentiated into three subjective sources of knowledge: sense, imagination, and apperception. In the transcendental subjectum, together with the affinity and the categories of which this subjectum consists, apperception becomes the ultimate forum of validity, lawmaking, and cognition. The phases of transcendental deduction are not psychological facts for Kant, but apriorities of validity. In spite of that, this is undoubtedly a lasting Kantian contribution to psychology. But for the time being their value is restricted to the demonstration of the multiple nature of the concept of association. What psychological realities they correspond to beyond their doubtless speculative origin has not even been indicated by investigations of modern psychology. Lewin's associational researches have justified Kant's findings only on two points: (1) The structure of associations is more delicate than was supposed by associational psychologists; (2) Lewin also found a basic condition which is the foundation of the production of associations which he termed *Tätigkeitsbereitschaft* (readiness for action).

But Kant's transcendental deduction is significant for associations from yet another angle. We have shown (section III) that Kant solved Hume's problem by introducing the categories. According to him the valid connections that arise through associations come about on the levels of categories. And transcendental deduction has shown by what process the "manifold" reaches the levels of the various categories contained in the transcendental subjectum. Modern psychology cannot make much of these categories, for its very point of departure was the liquidation of *Erlebnispsychologie*. The sharply distinguished steps of categories and deduction create the impression of Aristotelian crystal spheres, which do not take notice of the dynamic nature of psychic life whose play of forces cannot tolerate such rigid systems.

Kant, who limited the realm of reason to experience, was accused by the rationalist Couturat of not trusting the power of the human mind. If not in the name of rationalism, certainly in the name of dynamic psychology, one could accuse him of this, for the categorizing Kant did not believe that without such forms we should be capable of the admirable achievements of experience and cognition. Yet undoubtedly Kant made way in these rigid forms for new findings; discoveries often are made while limping on such crutches.

And this new finding was to be a lasting core of Kantian psychology—namely, that knowledge bears the marks not only of the nature of the external object but also of the knowing subject and that it is just that knowing mind-subject which endows the world of external *noumena* with laws. According to Kant, the portion of cognition that is of this subjective origin is a necessary component of cognition. In this respect Kant's criticism is not psychological but transcendental. The preexperiential nature of his categories and intuitions is not genetically historical but logically a priori. On the other hand, psychologistic criticism endeavors to remove from knowledge those elements which represent the reality of the external world subjectively and inadequately. This difference was clearly pointed out also by Windelband. However, only Windelband emphasized that Kant—had his historical position made the question at all possible—would himself have certainly sided with those who trace apriority genetically, instead of allying himself with the advocates of innatism.

Yet the fact that his historical position did not permit him to formulate the question of the origin of apriority brought him into a paradoxical situation. It has been pointed out that the arbitrary arrangement of categories follows from this paradoxical situation. The complete examination of apriority could have been achieved only by a genetic examination, while Kant was obliged to hunt around for the a priori categories empirically.

Some of Kant's followers, among them Hegel and Feuerbach, attempted a historical examination of apriority. They arrived at the conclusion that man and all that is peculiar to him are created by the reciprocal action between him and his environment and that makes him what he is. Thus is created everything we call apriority. But in this context genetic examination of apriority explodes the proposition that reason bestows law on the universe. The a priori forms and concepts in the intellect which embody the law have themselves developed historically—namely, they were produced in man's reciprocal relations with nature, the external world.

The genetic analysis of apriority left the two main pillars of criticism untouched: (1) reason can be exercised only within the realm of experience, (2) cognition is composed of subjective and objective elements. But since he viewed apriority as genetically created, Kant placed the basic principles of lawmaking in the processes of nature, the external world.

And thus cognition, which, for Kant, is a subsumation into a priori categories in the transcendental subjectum, became, in critical psychologism, the history of man's development, his formation by nature. In this history, the human mind is a product of the external world, but this molding external world produces it only insofar and inasmuch as the mind perceived it in an earlier stage. Yet mind is essentially different from the external world because, contrasted to the *plurality* of the world, it is *unique* and as such it can reflect the other only symbolically. This holds even if, with the development of the human mind, this symbolism becomes more and more adequate. In modern psychology this developmental process was outlined by Piaget, who wrote a penetrating criticism of the principle of apriority, based on the findings of child psychology.

VI

We have seen the relationship Kant established between sensation and reason. But it has to be pointed out that with the above assertions Kant did not yet consider the relationship between sensation and reason clarified. He still felt that between the two, between the "manifold" and the categories, there is still a gaping abyss; so he added to his system some further elements between these two.

In the schematism of pure reason, he strove for the establishment of such sensory conditions as would render the pure a priori concepts applicable to the data of the senses, to the "manifold." The scheme, according to him, depicts that general procedure of the imagination by which it creates the image of a concept. Accordingly, it is the model of every possible experiential object. Thus it is a true mediator between sensation and reason. It is no longer the raw material of the "manifold" but the manner of functioning of one of the cognitive forces, so that the pure a priori concept is now applicable to it, for qualitatively they are the same. The significance of the scheme as regards associations, emerges when we compare it with Hume's "associations by resemblance," in which not only concepts but also the intellectual processes giving rise to them are associated. But we do not have to appeal to Hume. It is our everyday experience that it is not the association of a word or concept which guides our imagination, but a similar procedural scheme of our own intellectual activity that helps find the required concept. Frameworks of intellectual functions, familiar to the speculative thinker, which, shadow-like, precede the concepts, are particularly well known. These frameworks evoke the concepts in the same manner in which the concepts evoke the referents they represent.

In the system of the maxims of pure reason Kant collected those fundamental synthetic propositions that directly originate in the categories.

He tried thus to bring together the two worlds from both the sensory and the intellectual side. The maxims—axioms, anticipations, analogies, and postulates—begin from the categories to carry out the task that had been done by the schema via the empirical procedure of the imagination. These four maxims express the norm to which we usually refer our associations. Especially analogies and anticipations are our everyday experience. Kant supplied us the further framework of the delicate structure of associations in them.

The detailed analysis of the schema and of the four maxims has far-reaching epistemological requirements which we have to forego. These problems are equivalent to that of object formation and concept formation and were treated above in connection with other authors. Here, too, Kant attempted to capture the processes and secure validity by aid of a rigid disposition of elements.

In this connection we have yet to point out that Kant gave evidence of that thread of the history of the concept of association that goes back to Bacon; namely, that associations are sources of error. This is contained in the section entitled *The Amphiboly of Reflective Concepts* of the *Critique*. According to Kant, the source of amphiboly is that

. . . if with these concepts we wish to proceed to the objects themselves, a transcendental reflection is necessary first of all, in order to determine whether they are meant to be objects for the pure understanding or for sensibility. Without this reflection, our use of these concepts would be very uncertain, and synthetic propositions would spring up which critical reason cannot acknowledge, and which are simply founded on transcendental amphiboly . . . [(19) 2, 3, Appendix].

In our terminology this must be expressed as follows: inasmuch as we attribute the connections fortuitously created by sensation to pure reason, there arise so-called synthetic maxims; these however are false. On the other hand, if we attribute the propositions created by reason to sensation, we again arrive at amphibolies. It need not be demonstrated that here again we are dealing with their various levels, which—even after the establishment of categories—always have to be actively pondered.

It may also be shown that the dialectic inferences of pure reason, paralogisms, antinomies, and ideals also stem from the fact that we transfer modes of inference that arose under one set of conditions to other types of concepts; that is to say, we associate them incorrectly. But the demonstration would again transcend the boundary of our investigations.

VII

Kant deduced the categories of pure reason, which make the general validity of a priori synthetic judgements possible, from various types of judgement. At this point our problem touches the question of the power of judgement. This connection was not worked out by Kant in detail, for he sharply separated pure reason, the power of judgement, and practical reason, allowing only that the power of judgement is an intermediary between pure reason and practical reason, between law of nature and law of freedom. We too should like to point out only the fact of that connection and the relationships springing from them.

According to Kant, the power of judgement is generally understood to be the ability to perceive the specific as contained in the general ([20] Introduction, IV). Then he points out that this function of the power of judgement necessarily has to rest on an a priori principle and demonstrates that this a priori principle is purposiveness ([20] Introduction, V). Finally he shows that purposiveness is coupled with intent directed at knowing. But the fulfillment of all intent is connected with the feeling of pleasure (lust) ([20] Introduction, VI). Thus, pleasure and pain (the determining causes of the power of judgement), the ability to know (the determining cause of reason), and the capacity to desire (the determining cause of practical reason), are all placed side by side (21').

But the categories cause the general validity of judgements and are themselves deduced from types of judgement; and since this proved to be identical with the problem of the general validity of associations, it is possible to work out the connection between the factors in the drive dynamism of pleasure and pain on the one hand and judgements, validity, and the intellectually cognitive role played by associations on the other.

That this possibility in the Kantian system is not a forced interpretation is witnessed to by yet another connection. We have seen that Kant based each step in the gradual process of the transformation of the "manifold" into experience on the unity of the self, or transcendental apperception. On the other hand, since he attributed three basic capacities to that self—knowing, pleasure-pain, and ability-to-desire—it is clear that the "manifold" which enters into the unit of the "self," into apperception, has to bear the mark of all three capacities of cognition, among them the capacity to feel pleasure and pain, which corresponds to the power of judgement (21').

We see that the connection we have always tried to seek out between the associative function of reason and man's drives or impulsive tendencies is present also in Kant, though the structure of his rationalistic system keeps the poles of this relationship apart. Kant did not further develop that thought. He accepted apperception, pure reason, and categories unquestioningly, just as he had accepted Aristotelian logic, never searching for their origin or their connection with the dynamism of human desires. He accepted them in order to use them for his purpose. Although the dynamism of desire is mentioned in connection with the critique of the power of judgement, and some light is shed even upon the connection between associations and the dynamism of desire, this line of thought remained necessarily unfinished.

VIII

In Kant's doctrine, not only baroque philosophy but also the epistemological influence of associations reached its climax. Everything that happened after him in philosophy as regards the problem of associations is merely the polishing of one or another element of Kant's synthesis and its remodeling according to the authors' experiences or philosophical penetration.

In the next period, the examination of associations is taken over by the just-born experimental psychology, inheritor of associational psychology, where it becomes shallower but is then again deepened by various schools of modern psychology.

After Kant's synthesis only new empirical research, new data, can lead to a new formulation of the problem of association, to a new solution and new perspective of the question of existence and consciousness in philosophy and epistemology. This aim is being pursued in our day, and around it schools and directions are grappling with the task, just as they were in Kant's time. The time for synthesis has apparently not yet come.

Summary

INVESTIGATIONS OF conceptual history will be summarized from three angles: (1) Development of the concept of association and of the problem of being and consciousness; (2) formulation of the unity of psychology, of the psychic law; (3) the genesis of the present-day concept of association. At the end of the summary, I shall indicate the direction of further development as far as it is predictable today.[1]

1. In this epoch the conceptual history of association progressed parallel with the fundamental problem of epistemology, the problem of being and consciousness.

Bacon's empiricism made associations a source of error stemming from human nature.

Descartes' skeptical rationalism and the duality of body and soul in his doctrine exploited the role of associations, attributing great importance to them.

Hobbes' sensualistic nominalism, the doctrine that truth is found in sensation, was based upon the mechanism of associations.

Spinoza's mystic rationalistic pantheism was made pos-

---

[1] *Editorial note:* See also "The Recent History of the Association Concept" (1938). In: *The Collected Papers of David Rapaport,* ed. M. M. Gill. New York: Basic Books, 1967.

sible by the doctrine of the unity of body and soul, the elevation of associations to the role of law.

Locke's sensualistic empiricism, the sensation-reflexion formula, lost its rigidity through the examination of associations and gave rise to genetic empiricism.

Leibniz's rationalism sought to comprehend the emerging unity of reason and cause, the phylogenesis of the consciousness of monads, by means of associations.

In *Berkeley*'s solipsistic world, ideal existence had associations play the role of law and providence.

Hume's skeptical-empirical view has associations produce the forms of cognition. The principle of uniformity in the processes of nature make Hume an empiricist, the subjective-associational generation of cognitive forms made him the father of positivism.

Kant's transcendental critique is occasioned by the fundamental question of the validity of associations. By means of the associations made on the levels of the categories, the subjectum makes the laws of the world of objects.

2. The conceptual history of associations also runs parallel with the development of the conception of psychic unity and the uniform psychological law.

In *Bacon*, the psyche appears only as a setting of idols and negatives.

Decartes split the psychic realm into two antonomous domains, reason and the soul (*les esprits animaux*), the latter being under the influence of the body. Association becomes the law of psychic life. But this can be accomplished only by shutting reason out of the psychic realm. Thus is born the first system of the psychology of consciousness, while reason is treated as an innate principle independent of the soul.

Hobbes takes over the Cartesian inheritance. He crystallizes the psychic domain into uniform mechanical law. His sensualism avoided Descartes' problem of reason, but his mechanistic conception forces him to shut the obscure and mechanistically unmanageable soul out of his framework of psychological law.

Spinoza unifies the laws of the world of consciousness and of the extended world. For him both laws are identical with associations. This mystical, imponderable solution realizes the all-embracing psychic law for the first time. But this law can hardly be called a psychological one.

Locke brings a new point of view to the developing psychic morphology. He spells out the necessity of genetic examination. He takes a first step toward subjecting to a uniform law healthy versus morbid and normal versus abnormal psychic data, by means of genetic examination.

Leibniz takes over Locke's genetic viewpoint and outlined the phylogenesis of the psychic process. His system designated the place of the unconscious mental activity. His method is genetic; it binds reason, cause, and association together in a phylogenetic unity and does not exclude any part of the psychic realm from the psychic law he creates. For that very reason, he is the first to lay a harmonious psychological foundation.

In *Berkeley*, sensualistic psychology falls back to the level of Hobbes' association mechanism. In the world of this solipsistic idealism, associations become a ruling principle of law; yet this law, like Spinoza's, can no longer be called a psychological one.

Hume worked out the topography of associational mechanism to a point where the accumulated material broke through the confines of mechanism. The skeleton constructed by his predecessors is given flesh and blood in his system—the possibility of uniform psychic law. With him, the unity of the mind is not a program but a reality. For him, the problem of knowledge was also a purely psychological question. He does not propose to decide between "truth" and "falsehood" but asks *why* we see phenomena the way we actually do. In Hume's investigations we behold the new perspective in psychology.

Kant replaced Hume's psychology with the examination of the a priori conditions of knowledge. He was not interested in the psychological question. Nevertheless his work became the foundation for the epistemological aims of psychology.

3. The course of development of the concept of association is as follows:

In *Bacon* associations are mere sources of error. Bacon tried to eliminate them and created the method of induction.

Descartes considered associations as sources of error; they led him to skepticism. At the same time he described their mechanism. Instead of them, Descartes chooses the innate ideas as the source of knowledge.

Hobbes completely works out the mechanism of associations as the determiner of all mental processes, except for unordered associations.

Spinoza's mechanistic associational law embraces the entire world of being and consciousness.

Locke finds that associations are the essence of reflection and intuition, and consequently of the formation of concepts and objects. The concept of association loses its mechanical character. From the error-inducing role of association, the *associatio idearum* was born. He recognizes the flight of ideas as also a result of associations. The examination of the nature of reflections, hence of associations, gives rise to the emphasis on the genetic method.

Leibniz applies the genetic method to the examination not only of concepts, but also of the nature of thinking and of logic in general. He is prompted by this to regard associations as an earlier stage of logic and thinking. He develops an antimechanistic concept of associations, which intimates the unconscious in the "petites perceptions."

Berkeley assigns a mechanistic activity to the associations, but he does not work out the mechanism in its details.

Hume's mechanism of associations again meets the genetic method; it becomes ramified, acquires dynamic qualities which break through the boundary of mechanism.

Kant's system deals with associations in two ways. On the one hand, empirical association is considered to be the mode of functioning of the imagination. On the other hand, on the levels of the categories, of pure a priori concepts, the associations gain validity and appear as a priori synthetic propositions. The relationship between categories and the "manifold," that is to say transcendental deduction, shed light on the structure of associations.

To this outline of the development of the concept of association, it should be added that—as already Descartes knew—the emergence of associations is determined by curiosity, by interest—in a word, by desires. We have found that thought in each of the philosophers discussed.

Locke and Leibniz deepened its meaning by the concepts of uneasiness and appetition. Hume built up a dynamism of desires, on the conditions of the production of associations. We have found the core of that conception in Kant.

This conception may rightly be regarded as the guiding thread in the history of the concept. We have repeatedly pointed out in our discussion that the latest investigations in modern psychology have forced us to resume the same thread. The exploration and exposition of that thread established the historical continuity between the concepts of association of psychology as part of philosophy and as an independent discipline.

In the development of the sciences, historical continuity is more than a descriptive methodology. It is the foundation and the begetter of all those hypotheses with which we face new investigations so they may yield up the secrets of nature and of human existence.

A systematic continuation of the history of associations is sure to serve as a basis for fruitful hypotheses.

Reference Notes

(1) Cassirer, E. (1906), *Das Erkenntnisproblem in der Philosophie und Wissenschaft der neueren Zeit,* I & II. Berlin. *Problem of Knowledge: Philosophy, Science, and History Since Hegel.* New Haven: Yale University Press.

(2) Descartes, R. (1650), Traité des passions de l'âme. In: *Oeuvres de Descartes,* ed. J. Simon. Paris: Charpentier, 1850. The passions of the soul. In: *Descartes Selections,* ed. R. M. Eaton. New York: Scribner, 1927.

(3) Descartes, R. (1637), *Discourse on Method.* LaSalle, Ill.: Open Court.

(3′) Descartes, R. (1701), *Regulae ad Directionem Ingenii.* Opuscula Posthuma Physica et Mathematica. Amsterdam. *Rules for the Direction of the Mind,* trans. L. J. Lafleur. Indianapolis: Bobbs-Merrill.

(4) Descartes, R. (n.d.), *The Method, Meditations, and Philosophy of Descartes,* trans. J. Veitsch. New York: Tudor.

(5) Windelband, W. (1911), *Geschichte der neueren Philosophie,* I. & II. Leipzig. *History of Philosophy,* I & II. New York: Harper & Row, 1968.

(6) Bacon, F. (1620), Novum Organum. In: *Great Books of the Western World,* XXX. Chicago: Encyclopaedia Britannica, 1952.

(6′) Bacon, F. (1623), *De Augmentis Scientiarum.* London, 1857. *Advancement of Learning.* New York: Dutton.

Editorial note: The references presented by David Rapaport in the original Hungarian text were to early foreign-language editions and were often incomplete. Wherever possible, additional information and references to English-language editions have been supplied.

(7) Fracastoro (1555), *Turrius Sive de Intellectione*. Venice: Opera, pp. 165–170.

(8) Telesio, B. (1588), *De Rerum Natura Juxta Propria Principia*. Tractationum. Phil. I (no locus).

(9) Locke, J. (1690), *An Essay Concerning Human Understanding*, I, ed. A. C. Fraser. New York: Dover, 1959.

(10) Locke, J. (1690), *Essay Concerning Human Understanding*, II, ed. A. C. Fraser. New York: Dover, 1959.

(11) Leibniz, G. W. (1714), The Monadology. In: *The Monadology and other Philosophical Writings*, trans. R. Latta. New York: Oxford University Press, 1898.

(12) Leibniz, G. W. (1703), *New Essays Concerning the Human Understanding*. La Salle, Ill.: Open Court.

(12') Leibniz, G. W. (n.d.), *Kleinere philosophische Schriften*. Leipzig: Reklam Univ. Bibl. *Philosophical Writings*. New York: Dutton.

(13) Leibniz, G. W. (n.d.), Principles of Nature and Grace Founded on Reason. In: *The Monadology and Other Philosophical Writings*, trans. R. Latta. New York: Oxford University Press, 1898, pp. 405–424.

(13') Leibniz, G. W. (n.d.), *Quid Sit Idea*, VII, p. 263. Paris: Gerhardt, 1875–1890.

(14) Leibniz, G. W. (n.d.), Correspondence with Arnauld. In: *Leibniz*. Trans. G. R. Montgomery. LaSalle, Ill.: Open Court, 1950.

(14') Leibniz, G. W. (1710), *Theodicy*. New Haven: Yale University Press, 1952.

(15) Berkeley, G. (1709), New Theory of Vision. In: *Berkeley Selections*, ed. M. W. Calkins. New York: Scribner's Sons, 1929, pp. 1–98.

(15') Berkeley, G. (1744), *Siris, A Chain of Philosophical Relections*, ed. M. W. Calkins. New York: Scribner's Sons, 1929.

(15") Berkeley, G. (1705–1708), *Commonplace Book*. Fraser, 1871.

(16) Berkeley, G. (1710), Treatise Concerning the Principles of Human Knowledge. In: *Berkeley Selections*, ed. M. W. Calkins. New York: Scribner's Sons, 1929, pp. 99–222.

(17) Hume, D. (1739), *Treatise of Human Nature*. Oxford: Clarendon, 1888.

(18) Hume, D. (1748), An Enquiry Concerning Human Understanding. In: *The English Philosophers from Bacon to*

Mill, ed. E. A. Burt. New York: Modern Library, 1939, pp. 585–689.

(18′) Hume, D. (1748), On Passions. *Essays Moral, Political, and Literary*. New York: Oxford University Press, 1963.

(18″) Hume, D. (1777), *Essays and Treatises on Several Subjects*. London.

(19) Kant, I. (1781), *Critique of Pure Reason*. London: Macmillan, 1963.

(20) Kant, I. (1788), *Critique of Practical Reason*. New York: Bobbs-Merrill, 1956.

(21) Kant, I. (1798), Anthropology of Immanuel Kant. *J. Speculative Philos.*, 9 (1875):16–27, 239–245, 406–416; 10 (1876):319–323; 11 (1877):310–317, 353–363; 14 (1880):154–169; 15 (1881):62–66; 16 (1882):47–52, 395–413.

(21′) Kant, I. (1794), Über Philosophie überhaupt. In: *Kleine logish-metaphysische Schriften*. Leipzig.

(22) Révész, G. (1917), *Leibniz pszihilógiája*. In: Leibniz Emlékkönyv. Budapest.

(23) Hobbes, T. (1650), *De Corpore Politico*.

(23′) Hobbes, T. (1658), De Homine. In: *Man and Citizen: De Homine De Cive*, trans. B. Gert. New York: Doubleday, 1972.

(24) Hobbes, T. (1651), *Leviathan*. New York: Oxford University Press, 1909.

(25) Spinoza, B. (n.d.), *Short Treatise on God, Man and His Well-Being*. Plainview, N.Y.: Russell, 1963.

(26) Spinoza, B. (1677), Ethics. In: *Chief Works*, II, ed. & trans. R. H. Elwes. New York: Dover.

(27) Freud, S. (1900), The Interpretation of Dreams. *Standard Edition of the Complete Psychological Works of Sigmund Freud*, IV & V. London: Hogarth Press, 1953.

(28) Gelb, A. (n.d.), Farbenkonstanz der Sehdinge. In: *Bethe-Bergmann Handbuch der gesamten Physiologie*, XII, 1.

(29) Hissmann, M. (1777), *Geschichte der Lehre von der Assoziation der Ideen*. Göttingen.

(30) Klemm, O. (1911), *Geschichte der Psychologie*. Leipzig-Berlin.

(31) Köhler, W. (1923), Zur Theorie des Successivvergleiches und der Zeitfehler. *Psychol. Forsch.*, 5:115–175.

(32) Lange, F. A. (1866), *A History of Materialism*. New York: Harcourt, Brace, 1925.

(33) Lewin, K. (1922), Das Problem der Willensmessung und der Assoziation *Psychol. Forsch.*, 1:191–302; 2:65–140.

(34) Werner, H. (1933), Einfuehrung in die Entwicklungspsychologie. Leipzig. *Comparative Psychology of Mental Development.* New York: International Universities Press, 1948.

(35) Wulf, F. (1922), Beiträge zur Psychologie der Gestalt: Über die Veränderung von Vorstellungen. *Psychol. Forsch.*, 1:333–373.

Library of Congress Cataloging in Publication Data

Rapaport, David.
The history of the concept of association of ideas.

Translation of Az asszociacio fogalomtörtenete, which was originally
presented as the author's thesis, University of Budapest, 1938.
   Bibliography: p.
   1. Association of ideas.   I. Title.
BF365.R3613   150'.19'2   73–89438
ISBN 0–8236–2330–0